God's Destiny

FOR LIL' DUKE

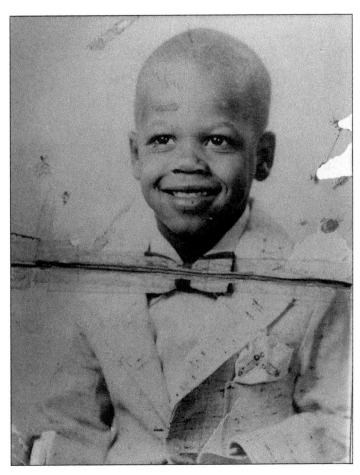

Me at five years old.

God's Destiny
FOR LIL' DUKE

by

WALTER DUKES, JR.

XULON PRESS

Xulon Press
2301 Lucien Way #415
Maitland, FL 32751
407.339.4217
www.xulonpress.com

Unless otherwise indicated, Scripture quotations taken from the
King James Version (KJV) – *public domain.*

Printed in the United States of America.

Paperback ISBN-13: 978-1-6628-1000-8
eBook ISBN-13: 978-1-6628-1001-5

THIS BOOK IS DEDICATED to the following people, who have played an important part in my life, and have guided me in developing into the man that I am today. I want to thank them, both living and dead.

1. My great grandmother, Florence Johnson. She took me in at the age of two years old and raised me until the age of fourteen years old. She taught me good values, such as work ethics, taking responsibility for one's actions. She taught me how to clean, wash, and iron. Also she introduced me to Jesus at a very young age. Thank you Gramma! I only wish that she could have seen how I turned out as a man, a husband, father, and most of all a man of God. Rest in peace Gramma!
2. My father, Walter Dukes Sr. He took me out of my home town, just in the nick of time, and saved my life from the direction that I was headed in. And because of him, I was able to meet the sunshine of my young life. Dad you died at such a young age, and you didn't have a chance to see your eldest boy grow into the man that I am today. But I thank you and miss you as well!
3. My mother, Isia Mae Pringle, as well as Henry Pringle her husband. My mother would tell me about having a relationship with The Lord every time that I would go to visit her and Pop. She would say sonny, why don't you stop what you

are doing and serve the Lord. This is what she would say every time that I visited her house. So because of her prayers and little talks, I'm saved today. Pop was a great influence on me, helping me with my integrity and preaching the truth that helped me turn to Jesus. Pop died at a very young age as well. Fifty six years old. Gone but not forgotten. I still think of him.

4. My godfather, Hersey L. Taylor. After Pop died he took me under his wing and mentored me in the preaching of the gospel, and how to navigate through the ranks of the church. How to interact with the members of my ministry and a host of other things pertaining to ministry. We traveled together on so many occasions. He and mother Taylor taught my wife and I so many good things. Thank you, Mom and Pop Taylor.

5. My daughters, Quanika Dukes-Spruill and Ishia Dukes-Davis. They inspired me to write this book on my life. There are events of hurts and pains that I didn't mention here because they would not be edifying to the reader. Hurts and pains that these two young ladies ministered to me on and helped me get through some very dark days. I love my daughters immensely. A father couldn't ask for better then these two ladies, both educators. My daughter Quanika for her help in the editing process and Ishia for her inspiration to write this book. I love you both very much!

6. My first love, and devoted wife of 46 years until her passing, Gracie Mae Dukes, the mother of my only two children. If it wasn't for her coming into my life at such a young age, and unwavering love, I don't know how I would have turned out. What a woman! God knew exactly who I need and why I needed such a strong woman in my life to help me mature into a man's man. She was so strong and I know that she

loved her family so much. She called Quanika, Lady and Ishia, E. Those nick names stuck with her until she passed in 2017 one day before our forty seventh wedding anniversary. I miss you, Honey. Rest in peace!

7. And last but not least, my wife, Joan Lavern Covert. You entered my life at a time that only God could orchestrate and at a time when the love that you provided was essential. I appreciate your continued support and devotion. Without your encouragement, this book would not be possible.

Chapter One

My life began on May 24, 1951. I was born and raised in the oldest town in the Louisiana purchase, called Natchitoches; pronounced Nack-ku-tuch. In the section of town called Bailey Heights, the roadways were made of dirt and the community was comprised of poor white and black people. Although there were several "Mulatto" families, they were often referred to as *black*. The population of Natchitoches at the time of my birth was approximately 9,415 residents. All nine-thousand-plus of us lived in a poor community. Amenities and simple necessities of which we are now accustomed were neither plentiful nor available to blacks at that time. The houses in my hometown were mostly made up of houses where you could stand on the front porch of the house, and if the door was open, could look straight through the house and see the backyard, called *Shot Gun homes*.

Residents of Bailey Heights used home remedies for ailments and sickness. Doctors were not plentiful and Black could not go to the local hospital in Natchitoches. There were two doctors in town, Dr. Cook and Dr. Seals, white physicians who would treat the blacks well. However, most Black people could not afford to go to the doctor in that era. Pine resin for the throat aches, and for the flu, you'd would use castor oil and black draw, these were laxatives, to flush out any germs that caused the ailments.

My introduction to this world was unique as I was delivered by my father's grandmother. My great grandmother, who I loving referenced as *Grammo*. *She* was a midwife in town and actually delivered many Bailey Heights babies. My parents, Isia Mae Washington and Walter Dukes, were not married. I was the fourth born to my mother who already had three children. My eldest sister Donnell, sister Dorothy, and my older brother, Donald Ray, came before me. I came out a little red-haired baby boy with a reddish complexion. They nicknamed me Li'l Duke. I can remember sleeping in bed with my entire group of siblings. In the morning, I would awake with a foot in my face or something else intruding on what little personal space I claimed. A small house with four kids was the order of the times.

My father had gone off to the war in Korea. That left my mother and four children alone to fend for ourselves. We were very poor and often went hungry. I would sometimes, at the age of two years, walk a three-block distance to my great-grandmother's house to get something to eat. So, my mother decided to allow me to live with her – my father's grandmother. I continued living with her for years; she raised me until I was fourteen.

My great-grandmother was Irish. She brought me into her home to raise me as her own. This is something I will always love her for. She only had a second-grade education, but she had a God-given talent of being one of the best Midwives in Natchitoches Parrish. She delivered more babies than the hospital. Remember, this was the Jim Crow era in the south. Blacks were not able to go to the local hospital for any procedures. We had to travel sixty-two miles to Shreveport for medical services. My Grammo, as I called her, brought me into this world as well. I will never forget the things she would do for me. Oh, how she would make those delectable buttermilk biscuits and from-scratch pancakes as big as the skillet that she made them in. She was an excellent cook. I can recall, in autumn, she would preserve all kinds of vegetables and fruit from the trees on the property. Plums, pears, and peaches were abundant. When this preserving was taking place, the whole area in town was scented with whatever she was canning. We grew all kinds of vegetables, corn, tomatoes, beets, carrots, and other vegetables. All was put up for use during winter.

My Grammo taught me to have a good work ethic. When other children were playing, I was working in the garden, cleaning the chicken coop, planting flowers, or weeding them. Looking back, I really hated the work, but didn't realize that she was teaching me good work ethics, and for that, I thank her the most. At the age of five years, she took me on a long journey, by train, to California.

Oh, what a trip. I can recall the prep work, getting ready to travel. Tickets had to be purchased and there was food to be prepared. She boiled eggs, made fried chicken, and baked my favorite cake. Talking about that cream cake that she'd made from scratch, just thinking about it now makes my mouth water. I don't have the recipe for the cream cake, but sure would love to have it. As I stated, this was the Jim Crow south and even though she was Irish, I remained to them, a Negro. Because of my skin color, we couldn't enter the food car on the train.

What a trip. Through the mountains and valleys we traveled. On the bends of the rails, I looked out of the window to the end of the train and saw a trail of cars behind us. When we reached California, I told her that when I turned eighteen, I would return to California. It was the most beautiful place that I had ever seen. The Pacific Ocean, the mountains, even the palm trees intrigued me immensely. We arrived in Oakland,

California, and went to her niece's home. They were well off; they owned a grocery store. Then we went to her daughter's home in Emeryville. I guess we must have been there at least a month, then on to San Francisco to visit her brother, Uncle Levy. After visiting him for a few days, we headed back to Louisiana.

My Grammo gave me a better life than my siblings had. I'd see them from time to time, but didn't live with them anymore. One sibling was my sister Dorothy. She and I had a strong bond. For some reason, we bonded at a very early age, but then one day, she was gone. She and my oldest sister had the same father. He arrived at Mom's house one day, all the way from California. He took Dorothy back with him. She would never again live with us in Natchitoches.

I missed my sister.

I would go to my mother's house on occasion to play with my siblings, but every time I got there, they had some kind of conflict going on. When I was five, my Grammo enrolled me in a Catholic school because I knew how to read and knew the alphabet. She wanted me to get the best possible education. She also didn't want me to walk the distance to the school, so she asked an older boy to walk with me. His name was Charles Davis. She rewarded him by feeding him breakfast with me, and then off we would go.

About that time, my step-great-grandfather had a stroke. As a result, he was paralyzed on one side of his body, and soon after, he passed. After his death, things really got hard for Grammo. She had to manage on just her income. My father owned the lot next to her property and she put a small one-room house on the lot. This house was purchased by my Grammo, and I was too young to know how she got it. However, I remember the truck and men bringing the house down the street. They pushed the electrical wires up with a pole, so the roof of the house would clear the wires. This was an exciting thing to a small boy. Soon she rented it to a man who called himself a prophet, and he would have church services there.

One night, my grandmother noticed that he would give all of the children a piece of candy except me. She approached him and asked why. He told her very loudly, "That boy is never going to amount to anything. He will make you cry and do very bad things, this is my reason."

Of course, his cruel words broke her heart and she cried. I looked up at him with tears in my eyes, not knowing how to respond to his words. Soon after, this my father came home from being stationed in New Jersey; I had not seen him since I was about three-years-old. I was about six at the time. This was the happiest day of my young life.

Dad had gotten married to a lady from Jackson Square. Her name was Genevieve Edwards. While my father was in Korea, my mother married another man and of course, this broke his heart. He'd told her, before going off to war, that when he returned, he would marry her, even with three children that were not his. When he came home, he found out that she was married to another man, and it wounded him so severely that he returned to the army and began drinking heavily.

So then he'd returned home for a visit. I was so excited to have my own daddy, and one that I didn't even know. He hugged me tight and said, "I'm your father." He and his wife stayed a few days with us. I can remember his wife had a special love for me; this made me feel so good. She took me downtown to the photo studio and had my picture taken. She dressed me up in a blazer and Bow Tie. Man, you couldn't tell me that I wasn't clean and sharp, even dapper.

After a few days, they were ready to depart. We all got in his brand new 1957 Ford Fairlane station wagon heading out of town. In my mind, I was on my way to New Jersey, not knowing that we were being dropped off in DeRidder, Louisiana to see Aunt Alice, my grandma's daughter, and her family. After a couple of hours, my father and stepmother were ready to pull out and proceed east to Jersey. So, I climbed in the car only to find out that I wasn't going with them.

This started me screaming and crying. I threw such a fit. I can remember the hurt that I felt when they pulled away. Brokenhearted, my grandma tried to console me, but to no avail. She told me that now, because her husband was dead, she needed me for company and a presence in her home. So, from that point, I would see my father only on occasion. Mostly, at Christmas time only. Even though my mother lived in the same town, I would see her from time to time, but there was no love for me pouring out from her. My grandfather and grandmother lived a couple of blocks from us. This was my mother's parents. I would go down to play with my aunts and uncles; also my cousins would join in. These were my mother's sister's children. Aunt Mary Louise was more of a mother to me than my birth mother. She had a heart of gold. She would feed me when I was hungry. I will always love her and cherish memories of her. My young uncle Richard Dale, Cousin Ezzard Charles, and I were very close in age; I was the oldest of the three, we would play and have fun together.

I didn't interact with my siblings too often. By this time, my mother had four more children, one by a man that she had earlier married, and three with a man she was not married to. Donald, my eldest brother, departed from our home town, with his dad. My next oldest sister, Dorothy, left town with her dad. Not knowing that I would not see her again until we were grown, she was eleven years old – she's four years my senior. I was heartbroken because we'd bonded at an early age. She was so beautiful, taking her beauty from our mother. I missed her immensely. Even though I had a better life than my siblings, I still loved them and wanted to be with them every chance that I had. Even though we had different fathers, we still loved each other, but I thought to myself, why wouldn't my father come to rescue me from this little town and take me back to New Jersey. My heart yearned for my daddy – didn't he love me?

Certainly, Donald was off to a better life. I missed him. One day they came back. I remember my brother all dressed up in new clothes and wore a watch on his arm. I was happy for him, even though we didn't live together, I would, from time to time, go and play with him. Now another sibling was gone. I missed my sister and brother.

I started wondering why my father wouldn't come and get me. Soon Christmas came around and Grammo told me that my father was coming home for Christmas. By now, I was in the fourth or fifth grade and no longer expected to go back with him. He arrived, but every time I'd see him, he was high or drunk from alcohol.

He'd told me that he had a real nice Christmas present for me. *Oh boy!* I was expecting to be blown away, so my imagination went wild. Christmas day came and I waited for him to show up. The afternoon came, and he showed up high and smelling of alcohol. He dug into his pocket and pulled out a wallet with a dollar in it and said, "Here, boy!"

I don't have to tell you that I was disappointed beyond measure. I took the dollar and asked my grandma if I could go to the movies. This was my escape from reality. Sometimes, I would stay and watch the movie two times. Once in a while, I'd watch it three times.

Dad departed and time marched on. By then, I'd started to feel my parents didn't love me. By the time I reached eleven or twelve, there was a day my grandmother called to the house and asked Grammo to send me down to the house. On the way, I wondered, *What do she want?* She'd never asked for me before. My mother's mother was a hard-working woman; she did the only job that was available to Black non-college-educated woman. That was domestic labor in the white people's homes. Cooking and cleaning their homes, and then go home to cook and clean their own homes.

My grandmother was an excellent cook. Wow, she would make meat pies from scratch, and sweet potato turnovers. Her fried chicken was so good that if you wanted to, you could eat the bones as well. Her cakes were out of this world. She'd make a cake called a jelly cake. The icing was made from apple jelly. Don't cringe, it was very good! On Saturdays, as we played outside, she and my grandfather. His name was Nathaniel Franklin Washington, they would go to the A&P to make groceries. When they would return, he would line all of the children up at the back door and make ice cream cones. Oh, this was a treat for us on those very hot Louisiana days. So you see, I do have some good memories from childhood.

My grandfather was a hard-working man, skilled in auto body repair. He was a very short man, but very strong and upright in character. Also, he sang in the church choir. The story goes that when he was a young man, a pig stepped on his foot, and he knocked that very large pig out with one punch. Oh! What a man. I can remember him coming home with a car that had been in a crash. He took his tools, sat on a stool and beat the fender into shape with his special hammer and other tools. He'd have us come into the house on rainy days and sit us down to hear him read a Bible story, mostly the Old Testament stories.

I was very close to my mother's people and have fond memories of my grandparents. My grandparents raised nine children on their meager salaries. The grandchildren would call my grandmother *Mom ole'* and grandfather, *Daddy*, because he was a daddy to most of us whose fathers were not around.

I had to digress from the narrative to give you a picture of my sweet grandparents.

So, I arrived there , at my Grandmother's and she said, "Li'l Duke, your Mother is gone". She got back with Sam Roque and moved to Memphis, Tennessee."

"What?" I said. "Gone"? "Gone to Memphis?" It was a complete shock to me. My mind reeled with the news.

She said, "Yes." Then she began telling me the woes of her daughter's life in this little town. Her face showed her sadness as she walked away.

I left the room, crying again, shattered again. When I returned home, my Grammo asked what happened. I told her that my mother had left town for Memphis. She didn't say anything, just sighed and walked away.

After that, I started rebelling against the one person who had taken me in. I've always loved clothes, and I would do any job to make a dollar. Picking cotton was one of the ways we as young children would make a few dollars. Picking a hundred pounds of cotton would pay three dollars. It would take all day to accomplish that hard feat. The sun in Louisiana was unforgiving. As I got a little older, my Grammo bought me a used lawnmower. It used more oil than gas. I would go around to white neighborhoods to ask if I could cut their lawns, some would say *yes*, others would call me the "N" word and say some other things to me.

Grammo had another daughter by the name of Eunice; she came back home from California and moved in with us. Eunice didn't like me much. In fact, she was downright mean to me. I guess it was because I lived with her mother.

About my other grandfather, my father's father. Well, I didn't have any relationship with him, even though he lived on Jackson Square, just a few blocks away. One day, I was out playing with Ricky and Ezzard. Grammo called and asked if I would come and go to the store for a neighbor. I came home and went next door. As I entered her yard and approached the door, I looked down on the ground, and there was a dollar coin and a quarter. *Wow I'd hit it big.* I put the money in my pocket and went in. I ran all the way to the store and came back with the goods. The neighbor gave me a dime for going for her. Wow, a dollar and thirty-five cents. *Man, I'm going to the movies.* On my way to the movies, I stopped by my mother's house and asked one of my siblings to go with me. They declined because of babysitting duties. Because I didn't tell my grammo about my finding the coins or where I was going. She started looking for me. She made inquiries of my relatives, then she got to my mother's house and my sibling told her that I had gone to the movies. So when I got home, she was waiting for me, and she was very upset.

Chapter Two

NOW REMEMBER EARLIER I'D stated that I started rebelling against her? She told me that my grandfather was on his way over to the house to beat me. I begged her, and told her that I found the money next door, but she insisted that I had stolen the money from her purse. He arrived with a three-foot long piece of a water hose in his hand. Now this was a man who'd never showed me any kind of love or affection, and now he was coming to beat the daylights out of me with a stiff water hose.

He sneered at me and said, "Lay down on this bench. I don't want to have to hold you down."

He hit me across my buttocks five times with all of his strength. I screamed in agony each time that he whacked me. The next day in school, I couldn't sit down for the pain. No child, no matter how mischievous he or she might be, could ever deserve such treatment – such child abuse. That beating caused a hate in my heart against him and deepened the rebellion in my heart for my grammo.

When I was in the ninth grade, my grammo decided to marry a deacon from the church that we attended. We moved out of our house to his house, back in the woods of Breda town. I didn't like it there; he had a decent house but no inside bathroom. My grammo didn't like it either. I had to catch the bus to school. It was a difficult time because the boys in that community decided that I didn't belong there.

So, the bullying started. Now I was a scrapper and wasn't afraid to stick up for myself. One day getting off of the bus, Johnny decided to start in on me, with his friends standing around watching. I looked on the ground and saw a brick. I picked it up and clocked him upside the head. He and his friends ran off. I noticed he was bleeding from his head and crying. I went home expecting to be in some kind of trouble. The next day at the bus stop, he was there but didn't say anything to me. I kept my eye on him and his friends. After school, while on the way home, I thought that I would have to fight with him and his friends, but instead, he got off the bus and ran home, never saying anything to me again.

I must digress here for a moment and go back away to my seventh birthday. One night, my Grammo and I attended a church revival at the Pentecostal church that she attended. When the preacher called for people who wanted to be saved, I went up to the front. Now earlier that day, I had been playing marbles with my friend from the neighborhood. My pockets were full of marbles, both front pockets. When the preacher prayed for me, I hit the floor like I had seen others do. Boy! Those marbles flew all over the floor. In those days, Pentecostal beliefs were that marbles were considered gambling. Well, the preacher told me to pick each one up and go to the back door and throw them out. I followed his instructions. The next day I went back to the church looking for my marbles, if my memory serves me right, I didn't find even one of them. I must have thrown them with an anointing.

But something happened to me on that church floor. From that point, I began to speak to myself of things that I know that God had put in my spirit and thought process. Remember what the so-called prophet said to my Grammo, that I would never be worth anything? Well, I began to say to myself, not anyone else, "When I get grown, I'm going to have a wife with two children, a good job, a nice car, and by the time I reach thirty, I will have a house." I will tell you the results later in another chapter of this book. When I turn ten, I asked my Grammo for a bike for Christmas, but she told me that she couldn't afford to buy me a bike. But I thought to myself, *She's kidding.*

During those days after my great-grandfather's death, money was very thin, so she really meant what she'd said. She had no money for a bike. Christmas day came and I got up early looking through the house. No bike. I went outside, looking under the rear of the house that was raised and elevated on pilings. No bike. Now I was very distraught. I moped around the house, very sad, and my Grammo saw my countenance and said to me, "Li'l Duke, why don't you go down and play with your cousins and uncles?" So I did. When I arrived at my grandfather's house, (my mother's father) all of the kids were playing in front of the house with their new toys. My uncle Ronald had a new guitar, Ricky got a new football uniform and the girls had dolls and other kids had different things. So, the custom was to ask, "What did you get for Christmas?" And I was asked, "Duke what did you get?"

I replied, "Nothing." My head hung low. But instead of laughing or making fun of me, which was the norm coming from my family. They began to bring their toys to me to play with. That made me feel really good. You see, I was the picked-on kid. Some of my cousins enjoyed tormenting me. Now after about an hour of play, and I'm feeling like a regular kid, the phone rang and my grandmother called me. She said that Mrs. Florence said to come home. This was my Grammo calling for me. I went home to see her standing on the front porch. I didn't know what to expect.

She said, "Li'l Duke, go up to Julius Aaron's hardware store. He is waiting on you."

This was Christmas day and all of the stores were closed. I ran all the way to the store, which was about eight blocks from my house. When I arrived, there he was standing in the doorway.

He said to me, "Boy, your grandmother loves you. I was having dinner with my family. If it was anyone else, this would not have happened."

There, in the corner, was a red and white Schwinn bike. It was the only one he hadn't sold because of all the bells and whistles that it had. It was loaded. There was a light on the fender, a horn on the tank, streamers coming out of the handlebars. And white rims. Oh, my goodness, what a beautiful bike. It was the best looking bike among all the children riding new bikes that day. By the way, in those days, if you had a bike, you were considered very lucky.

Mr. Aaron said, "It's yours."

My mouth dropped open. I stared at the Schwinn and couldn't talk. Of course, I soon got over that. Mr. Aaron helped me out the door and soon I was sailing down the street on the best bike in the world.

The first place I went to was my grandfather's house, where everyone was still playing. When I rode up, they all stopped playing and stared. One kid said to me, "Duke, whose bike is that?"

I answered, "It's mine."

Now, of course, they thought that I was telling a story, as was the saying back then. But after I kept saying that I'd just got it, finally they believed me! So here was one of the very special highlights of my childhood. My grandma sacrificed and purchased that bike for her Li'l Duke.

Summers brought hot and very humid weather. One Sunday, a friend of mine from school, and I decided that we would take a ride out to Gayville. Now, the people who lived there were not gay. It was the surname of everyone that lived in the community. A family-owned spread of land. It was about six miles out of town. Of course, I didn't get permission to go, I just went. When we arrived, they were having Sunday dinner. Aunt Eunice's pastor and family were there, and others, They were also members of the church and the pastor had invited them to dinner after church.

They said to us, " what are you boys doing way out here?"

We replied, "Just riding our bikes."

They fed us and later, we rode out in front of their house when my friend noticed some dark clouds looming overhead. That meant a summer rainstorm was coming. During the summer in Louisiana, they can pop up anytime and then ten minutes later, be gone with no trace of rain.

My friend said to me, "I'm going home."

I thought to myself, "The preacher is here and he will take me home."

Bad choice, a REALLY BAD CHOICE.

Remember Eunice? Well, the pastor did put my bike in the back of his station wagon and took me home. Eunice was standing on our front porch. I got out of the car and Grammo asked me where I had been. The pastor told her that I was out in Gayville with him and that I had ridden my bike out there. Well, you can only imagine what happened next. Eunice marched me right by where Grammo was sitting on the sofa and into the bedroom. She took a thick leather belt and commenced to beat me with intensity. She was a large-built woman and strong. She struck me so much that I stopped screaming and crying, and just laid there until she got tired of beating me. Yes, I had been wrong in doing what I did without permission. But this was – again – child abuse. To beat a ten-year-old boy until he stopped crying. *That's child abuse.* But you can see a pattern of disobedience and rebellion. The prophet said that I would be nothing.

Now back to where I digressed from earlier in my story. I was in the tenth grade, barely passing my grades. In the morning, I had carpentry and the afternoon I had English, math, and social studies. Sometimes I would skip school and hang out at a fellow classmate's house whose parents were working. One day, I ran into the same friend I'd ridden bikes to Gayville with. Earlier, he and I went up to Stephen's Supermarket to steal some candy. As we entered the door, the owner was in the back of the meat department, the cashier up front, no customers in the store.

Let me tell you this before going on. This is the store that my Grammo shopped at, and remember the grandfather that I avoided at all cost? He was the butcher there. Well, we put some candy bars up our sleeves and attempted to walk out, not realizing that the owner was watching us through an overhead convex mirror.

He beat us to the door and said to me, "Boy I should call the police on you, but because of your grandmother I won't. But get out of my store and don't ever come back!"

I was just grateful that my mean grandfather was not there. Now I worried. *Oh boy, I'm in trouble again.* I was always doing something to make the prophecy come to pass.

I turned fourteen, one of the youngest in my class in the tenth grade. After the candy bar episode, my Grammo was so tired of me and my shenanigans. By this time, Eunice had moved to her property in DeRidder, Louisiana. And my Grammo was older, so we didn't keep the chickens or the garden anymore.

In fact, there were many nights that if Aunt Mae, who was my mother's oldest sister, if she didn't feed me, I would go to bed hungry. My Grammo was tired of my rebellion. I didn't know that I was hurting her so much and I'm sure she thought about what the so-called prophet had said concerning me. She didn't attempt to punish me or anything like that. In fact, I had started what was called *sassing* her, talking back, being disrespectful to her, the woman who took me in at the young age of two. Back when no one else cared for this little red-headed boy.

As I look back now as an adult, I only wish she could have seen how I turned out. She was so upset with me that she packed a suitcase and put me on a Greyhound bus to Memphis. I had no money, no directions. She just wanted me to go. Oh, my Lord, what a big disappointment I must have been to her. Before going to Memphis, I had put a blazer, pants, shirt, and tie on lay-away at the men's store. A classmate and I had a little job every Wednesday afternoon. We would meet the truck from New Orleans that would come for the A&P store. We'd meet up with the driver and he would give us five bucks each for unloading the truck. So when I left town, I was upset for not being able to get my clothes out. I am a bit of a clothes hound and I felt sad. I didn't know what to expect in Memphis, but most of all, how would my mother feel about me just showing up? She didn't say goodbye to me when she departed town, so I was concerned about how she would respond to me just showing up unannounced. I was unaware that my Grammo had not gotten in touch with her. She just put me on the bus out of town. I arrived in Memphis at night, with no money, no directions for survival. I got in a taxicab with the address that she gave me, and instructed the driver to take me to this address. I arrived at the address and knocked on the door while the driver waited to be paid. A large, very dark man with red eyes came to the door, and I asked for my mother.

His reply was, "Ain't no Isia Mae lives here."

So, I asked, "Did you know where she lives?"

"No!" he barked.

So, I turned back to walk to the taxi, and the driver started using some very colorful metaphors. He got on his radio to dispatch and they told him to take me to the youth house, because I was probably a runaway. Arriving there, they questioned me as to where I was from and if I had run away from home. I told them what happened and that I was looking for my mother. They put my picture on T.V. and ads on the radio to help find her.

Arriving at the youth house, a very nice man asked me, "Where are you from? Are you a runaway?"

I told him that I was from Natchitoches, Louisiana and I was not a runaway. My Grammo sent me to find my mother.

He said, "Alright, give me your name and information and we will contact your grandmother."

After our talk, he allowed me to go to sleep in the rec room on a sofa. I can only imagine what she told him of all of my behavior and what trouble that I had caused her. The next day he said that they weren't able to get in touch with her and that I had to be locked up with the other bad boys. So for two weeks, I was treated as a runaway. After this experience, I started thinking that I needed to change my attitude and be more serious about school and making the right choices in my life. That time of being locked up did me a wealth of good, not seeing my family and friends. I came home a changed young man, but the wheels were already in play for my father to come and get me.

When I got back home, I returned to school and back to my little job of unloading the truck. After being locked up for two weeks in boys' detention, my attitude changed. I realized that I had to make some changes because I didn't want to go to jail or the youth house ever again. That experience in Memphis was enough for me. I went to school every day and worked at the movie theater part-time.

There was a girl in my class I liked. We started going places together. We met at the fair and took pictures together. I left one of the pictures in my shirt pocket and my Grammo found it during wash day. Grammo face turned red, ''Is this a grown woman's picture that I found in your shirt pocket?'' She waved the picture in my face. My brain froze up. I stood there blinking and stuttering, trying to come up with the correct answer.

"Answer me," she exclaimed. "I'm going to call her house, give me the number."

After giving her the number, she stomped off to the phone to call her mother. I froze in place, hearing her dial the number on the rotary phone, all four numbers. The angry words that she spoke about me and all of my antics, I knew that it was over between me and that young lady. My chances of having a girl-friend were greatly diminished.

My Grammo got off of the phone and said, "Boy, I don't know what I'm going to do with you."

My head dropped, eyes on my shoes, I blinked, willing back the tears. Oh boy, she thought that it was a grown woman. So she'd called the girl's house to see if I was lying about her age. The girl's mother told my Grammo that she had no business fooling around with boys, so that was the end of trying to have a girlfriend. In fact, when the young lady saw me in school the next day, she wouldn't even speak to me.

Christmas came and I found out that the store still had my outfit in lay-a-way. So I got it out and dressed to the nines on Christmas day. I had no girlfriend, so I went to the movies – my favorite place to escape. The new year of 1966 came and went. One day, during February, I was walking home across the field behind the house and I looked up to see my best friend, Duck, running towards me. His real name was Donald Metyor. He was mixed with Indian and French, and a couple of years younger than me.

I asked, "Man, where are you going?"

He attended the Catholic school that I'd attended in first and second grade, but the school was in the other direction. He exclaimed to me that he saw my father on the corner, drinking with the men up there. Right away, I knew what his purpose was. He'd come to take me back to Jersey. Wow! What joy filled my soul and body that day. We ran together to my house and he continued on to his. Going up on the porch, my Grammo met me and said, "Li'l Duke, your father is here to take you back to Jersey with him."

As I looked at her, I noticed she had a very sad look on her face, as if in regret for what was happening now and the finality of it. In a few hours, my dad showed up, half drunk. He talked with me about leaving with him. I had no idea that he didn't have the funds for our return trip to Jersey. So an argument started with him and Aunt Eunice. She'd come to town when she heard that he was there. She didn't care for my father at all because of his drinking escapades.

So by the second day, they worked it out with bus fare for both of us. We went to my high school to get transcripts for my new school in Jersey. This time I had the chance to say goodbye to my classmates. The principal let me go into all of my classes to say goodbye. There was this one girl who started to cry when I said that I was leaving to go live in New Jersey. Her name was Mary Beck. She was a very beautiful girl. This shocked me. I had no idea that she even knew that I existed.

Oh well, I'm on my way to Jersey, I thought. I went down to my grandfather's house to say goodbye to my family that was present, and they all said goodbye to me, hugged me, and talked about how I felt about leaving and going to New Jersey.

My teachers said some encouraging words to me, and we departed town. When we left the house, I looked back at Grammo, she was crying. It made me feel bad to see her crying over me. I had, after my time in the youth house, made some changes in my actions. On the bus, my father said that we were stopping in Alexandria to see our uncle William – he was Grammo's youngest son. His wife made us a few sandwiches, and then we departed on the long journey to New Jersey.

Chapter Three

BY THE TIME WE got to Mobile, Alabama, the food was gone. Plus, Dad had no money to buy food. I was very hungry all the way to New Jersey. I know my father got tired of me asking, *"Is we there yet?"* By the time we arrived in Baltimore, there was a delivery truck passing the bus that displayed pictures of pies on the side.

I looked at my dad and said, "Look at the pies, they look so good." I was starving. A few hours later, we reached New Jersey. We finally got off the bus in downtown Newark, New Jersey. Remember that where I had just come from, the temps were in the high 50s and 60s in February. It was 20 degrees here. I was freezing while we walked from Broad Street all the way up to Broome Street, about seven cold city blocks.

I looked up at a thirteen-story building and said, "Dad, this is where you live?"

He said, "Come on, boy, let's go."

All the way to the building, he walked so fast that I couldn't keep up with him.

"Come on, boy," he kept yelling.

We got inside; the apartment was on the fourth floor. My stepmother met us at the door and hugged me tight.

She said, "I know you are hungry."

I waited while she fixed me some eggs. After talking awhile, I met my sister, Roberta. She was named after my father's mother, who'd died when he was ten years old. Then, I met Cecil, my brother, and we went to bed. The next day I looked out the window and realized that I was on the fourth floor of this tall building. It was taller than any building in my home town. Thousands of people lived on top of each other. This was shocking to me. My dad took me to the high school the next day, and of course we walked all the way there, about a half-mile from the house.

When we arrived at the school, I looked up at the building. It sat on a hill with a whole lot of steps leading up to huge entry doors. I was overwhelmed by the number of students I saw in the hallways going into classrooms. Here I was, fresh from the south and the number of high school students there had been about 300 children or so. This new school had about that many – just in the graduating class. Needless to say, I was intimidated by the dress and speech of the kids.

After a few weeks, I begin to come out of my shell and participate in class and take part in classroom discussions. The kids laughed at my southern speech and my clothes. Remember, Newark at that time was known for the stylish clothes and stores. Wow, again, I was being picked on. Walking home from school by myself, with no friends yet, I decided to just stay in the house.

One night after going to bed, I woke up the next morning and looked out the window, which I did each morning. I got the biggest surprise. That night it had started snowing. I had never seen snow like this, we only had sleet on occasion in Louisiana and that was a big deal for us as children. The snow looked to be about ten or twelve inches on the ground.

I couldn't help but shout out to my young siblings, "Look at the snow coming down!"

They laughed at me. I didn't care. I sat at the window, happy that I didn't have to go to school that day. So after the snow stopped that afternoon, there were about twelve inches of the white stuff. I went outside where other children were playing in the snow. I didn't have any gloves and soon found out that snow is unforgiving without gloves, so I went back in and the moment I entered the house, my hands felt like pins and nails were hitting them. It was painful until they warmed up.

Oddly, this high school in Jersey had the same name as my school in Natchitoches, *Central High School*. This really surprised me and it made me feel a little more comfortable. One day, a group of young men were teasing me about my clothes, and another young man stood, waiting until they walked off.

He said to me, "Man, don't let these guys get under your skin. I will tell you how they are able to dress the way that they do. Every one of them have after school jobs, that's how they buy their clothes from upscale downtown stores."

His words rang a serious bell in my mind because I loved to dress. Summer rolled around and I had begun to make a few friends there in the projects – David Redd, Delmar Walker, Bruce Rutherford, and Snukkie. We played basketball in the playground. One day, I was walking downtown with my dad and there was a sign in the window of this shop, *Boot Black wanted*.

So I asked my dad, "What is a Boot Black?"

He said, "It's a person that knows how to shine boots and shoes."

We looked in the window at the place. "Do you think that you can do that?" Dad asked.

I said, "Yes." The reason I answered right away, was because there was a place downtown Natchitoches, where Black people could congregate, actually, it was the only place. It was called the Ape Yard. It was named that by the white merchants. There was a Black man that would sit in this little shack and polish shoes. They would look like glass when he finished. So I would stand in the doorway of the shack and watch him do his thing, so I learned from watching him and doing my own shoes.

We went inside and the man hired me to work as a boot black. There was another boy working there as well, so at first, I watched what he did prepping the shoes before starting the polishing process. I caught on right away to their method and began to make big tips from the police detectives and motorcycle cops that came every day from the first precinct down the street.

Remember the lay-a-way plan in my home town? Well, I found a store that would let me put clothes on lay-a-way and all summer, I would build up my wardrobe. By the time school started in September, I had a serious collection of duds. Now I was in the eleventh grade and my father's drinking had gotten worse. He was employed as a chef when he was working. So he worked at night, and would come home drunk 2:00 and 3:00 a.m. in the morning. I was his target.

He'd wake me up, slapping me around, saying, "Boy, I'm going to make a man out of you." He would make me stay up with him until he fell asleep in the chair.

Many nights, my stepmother would try and get him to stop harassing me. But to no avail, he continued. He would take me to the bar with him, trying to make me like him, a woman chaser and alcoholic. I hated this life. Then I would try and stay out of his way, hoping every night that he would come home sober. My hope would be shattered when I heard him key the door and come in, yelling and screaming at my stepmother. I would pray and hope that he would not come after me. No chance of that happening. I was next in line.

This behavior went on from the tenth grade until the twelfth grade. But one day, during the summer of '67, I was standing outside and a brown-skinned girl came into the building.

I asked David, "Man who is that?"

He replied, "Duke, her name is Gracie, but don't waste your time, she's not going to give you the time of day. She's stuck up!"

Well, that just made me more intrigued. One day I was catching the elevator and she came into the building from church. She wore a blue suit and matching blue hat. Wow, my heart melted. This girl, I definitely wanted to meet and talk with. As she approached the elevator, I asked her what her name was. She looked me up and down and got on the elevator. She said, "My name is Judy."

I said, "No it's not," but the elevator door closed in my face. From that time on, I was hooked. The summer burst into full bloom.

One night, we had a peaceful night for a change in the Duke's household; my father was home and not drinking. When he didn't drink, he was a nice person, even humorous. So as we watched T.V., we heard the most ungodly sound coming from outside. It sounded like a train derailing off its tracks, only louder. It was the riots of the summer of '67. Well, people were pulling security gates off of stores, breaking the glass and going in, looting the merchandise from within.

When they reached the liquor store and began to do the same, my father said to me, "Li'l Duke, go get me some liquor." This is not what I expected, it shocked me, that my father would send me out into this rioting and looting, it was appalling to me, but I went obeying him, scared out of my mind.

My stepmother tried to convince him not to send me out there, because now the police were in force up the street. The riot happened so fast that it caught the authorities by surprise.

So, they were ill-equipped to handle what was happening in the Black community. So, brave Lil' Duke, hit the street. The projects emptied out, every young person was outside, some looting, others just watching. I went across the street to the liquor store on the corner, but by the time I reached it, the store was mostly empty. All of the big bottles of liquor was gone, just that quick. So I grabbed a few small half pints, just enough that I could carry them back in case I was confronted by the police.

When I got back home and pulled out four little half-pints of different liquors, my father was mad, very upset. He said, "Boy, all that liquor in that store and all you brought me was this **&&^%#*."

I said, "Dad, this is all that was left."

So for the next few days, we saw the state police come, then the National Guard patrolled the streets. Some people got shot, some arrested. The city hospital had an inch of blood on the emergency room floor. What a bad experience. I saw the community go down as I watched from the windows, stores burned, high-quality furniture stores looted. Most of the businesses were owned by Jews and Italians.

When the riot was over, most didn't come back into the community, so the community of course, declined. Burned-out buildings and shells of others was the view from the windows of the projects. What had been a decent place to live turned into a war zone. Within a few weeks, things kind of returned to some kind of normal. By then, I had moved from the boot black job to being a busboy in a French restaurant on Route 22 Springfield, N.J. I would catch the bus to work and come home in the evening. When I would see that beautiful brown-skinned girl, my heart would melt. I found out her real name is Gracie. I would try and talk to her, but she had very little conversation for me.

I found out through one of my friends that she had a girl-friend in the building. Her name was Paula. Paula found out that I liked Gracie and began to speak to me. I would talk to her, telling her how much I liked Gracie, then she would convey this to Gracie. So Gracie would at least speak to me. I wanted to make her my girlfriend in the worst way. At that stage of my life, all I wanted was a girl that I could treat like a lady and she was it. But of all the girls who lived in this huge building, Gracie had my heart and I was bent on making her my girl. One day, I was sitting on the bench in front of the building, looking up and down the sidewalk. I had showered and gotten dressed, very dapper.

By this time, I was one of the best dressed young men in Central High. So there I was, sitting by myself, in front of this very large building, there was no one around, no children playing, not a soul. I was tired of going to the movies by myself and wanted so much to have a girl name Gracie for my girl-friend. Behold, out of the building came the two girls who I'd found out had been eyeing me from the window of the ninth floor and came down to talk with me. I was happy to meet them and found out that they were Gracie's cousins.

I asked them, "Where is Gracie?"

At her brother's house. She's 15, I'm 16

They replied, "Upstairs."

They departed and went back upstairs and came back with Gracie in tow. But she stayed only for a few minutes and went back into the building. I was so disappointed. Well, I went to the movies by myself. After talking with Paula again about her, one day Gracie came into view and I approached her. This time she didn't run away. She talked with me, but very sarcastically.

I said, "How's my chances of making you my girl?"

She said, "I will let you know."

Gracie and I started dating.

In the meantime, she found out that I was a senior at central. When we returned to school in September, I found out that she had said to Paula, "I'm going to go to his prom."

Since she was a sophomore that fall and I was a senior, well, that was enough for her to say *yes*, my chances were good, that we could date. She had in her mind that after the prom she would dump me. But that didn't happen. One night before school started, a party was going on in the building and I asked her if she would go with me. This was our first date. She said *yes*. So being from the south, I knew the proper thing to do was go introduce myself to her parents. So I went to the ninth floor and knocked on the door.

A lady came to the door and said, "Yes, young man?"

I said, "My name is Walter Dukes, Jr. and I'm here to take Gracie to the party downstairs."

Well, she was so impressed by my introduction that she said, "Come on in, she went to the store and will be back shortly."

When I entered the living room, there were two other ladies there. Someone asked me where I was from. I said, "Louisiana."

They said, "We knew you weren't from here. You have southern manners."

So they questioned me about who my parents were and what floor I lived on. Soon, Gracie darkened the door. When she saw me, she looked really upset and said, "Let's go."

I don't know if she was more upset that I came to her house or that her aunts were so intrigued by me. When we got into the hallway, she said, "Who do you think you are coming to my house? I thought that we were meeting at the party."

I said, "Introducing myself to your family was the proper thing to do."

So she said, "Let's go."

We went to the party and she went over to her friends and didn't stay with me very long. I asked her to dance and she did. Then, she returned to her friends. At the end of the party, it was time to depart. We both had a curfew. I took her to the elevator and pushed the button. I turned and didn't ask her if I could kiss her, I took a chance and just did it. Wow, she kissed me back. From that day I fell in love with her, hook, line, and sinker. Now she's my girl. I took her to Palisades Park in No. Jersey, we had so much fun and I could tell that she liked me a whole lot. We started dating just before school started and the summer was ending.

I brought her home to meet my parents and my father said to me, "You shouldn't get tied down with just one girl, sow your oats, date other girls." But his words went in one ear and out the other.

Gracie was my girl and that's that. One day I was standing near my little brother's and my room. My father came into the house, half high and started in on me, yelling and saying some pretty foul language. He headed toward me, through the hallway of the apartment. He had in his hand a piece of flag pole; he swung it at me and I jumped back. He hit the wall and put a dent in that cement wall. I looked at the dent and lost it. The next thing I knew, I hit my father. I struck him so hard that he fell backwards into the living room and fell into a chair. On my way out the door, I said to my father, "You are not going to hit me anymore." Now after coming down from the adrenaline. I thought to myself, *I hit my father! I can't go back there.*

I didn't have but a few bucks and a small paycheck in my pocket, so I went downtown to a small hotel and tried to rent a room. The manager said that he couldn't accept a third-party check. I turned and decided to go to New York, to one of the all-night movies on 42nd Street. After watching the movie over and over, I fell asleep for a little while with my feet up on the seat in front of me – for fear of the rats running around on the floor. Rats, not mice!

Morning finally came and I started back to Newark. Arriving home, I went in. He said to me, "Boy, I've been in a lot of bar fights but I have never been hit as hard as you hit me." That's all he said to me. I didn't respond.

My prom night, with my girl, Gracie!

Chapter Four

DURING MY UPBRINGING IN Louisiana, my grandmother taught me to honor my father and my mother. I felt so bad that I had hit my father.

Soon, school started again. I was a senior high school student and had passing grades. I can only imagine what I would have been able to accomplish in life if only I'd had parents like some kids had – loving, supportive, sober. But God still had His hand on me. Just before senior class pictures were taken for the yearbook, I was standing in the kitchen one day at the fridge and my father was upset about something. We had a little breakfront separating the kitchen from the living room. He pushed the top part over on me in the kitchen and it busted my lip at the corner of my mouth. Oh, it did bleed for a while, but it didn't seem to bother him. Violence was part of his everyday life.

I went to school the next day with a patch over the wound. When the photographer snapped the picture, I turned my head to the left so that the bandage wouldn't be seen, and sure enough, you can see just the edge of it in the photo. Every day, I would walk Gracie to school and back home, then go to work at the French restaurant. One day I saw her in the school hallway.

When she saw me, she said, "I was already on the way home. I see too much of you… maybe we should be just friends."

This hurt me to the quick but I agreed. "Okay, we see too much of each other. I will fix that." So, I started leaving for school early and miss her. After school, I would go home right away and then on to work. I didn't know that she had a weak heart from a childhood Rheumatic Fever attack on her heart. So they moved her to another high school that had an elevator. The school was an arts high school on High Street. Now she didn't see me at all. So after about three weeks of her going to the new school, she sent a message to me at Central via one of her old friends.

This was another girl friend of Gracie's who liked me as well, and she would let me know that by things that she'd do. But she gave me the message and, after school, but before going to work, I went up to her house. There Gracie was, looking so beautiful. She said *come in.* She had two of her friends there with her. I could tell by the way she'd answered the door that she missed me. It had been about three weeks since she had seen me. So she gave me a letter and expected me to leave. But I sat down and read it. She hadn't wanted me to do that in front of her giggling friends. I read it and said, "I will call you later on."

I went on to work. My little plan had worked well in my favor, but I know now that God was in the plan, not just my plan; it was God's. So now she would only see me on Sundays because if you know anything about French restaurants, Saturdays was the busy time and I had to work. I would get off work around 11 p.m. – too late to see her. So now her complaint was *I don't see you enough.* Man, women!

The prom plans were in full swing. I had my Gracie back and I was a happy young man. I had a very good friend in my English class; his name was Paul Ashford. We got together and rented a limo, it cost us $63.00 apiece. He had a job as well. We'd put our money together and rented a limo for our prom dates.

He dated Roslyn, a girl from Clinton Hill section of Newark. The time of the prom was so exciting for me; I now had a girl-friend, not just any girl. She was a virgin and very much in control of her emotions. I completely respected her and when she said *no*, I respected her choice and admired her for her strong will. So the night of the prom, the limo driver picked up Paul and Roslyn first and then on to us. I went up to Gracie's house and picked her up. Her uncle and aunt were guardians over her, since her parents were both deceased. They said how nice we both looked. We even matched. I had an ice blue dinner jacket with blue, ruffled shirt and black pants and bow tie. Man, I was dapper again. No one else at the prom had that jacket on.

Gracie had an ice blue evening gown on and we looked perfect together. Soon we were outside and the whole population of the projects was outside, hanging out the window yelling at us as if we were big-time movie stars. We felt like we were, especially since we had a white chauffeur. He got out of the car and opened the door for Gracie and me to get in. The people around the project building were so happy for us and showed us so much love.

Things were so different in those days, 1968. In my mind, I thought, as soon as I graduated school, I would join the Navy and leave my father behind. But it made me smile, knowing that I had a wonderful piece of sunshine to write to me while I'm away. We arrived at one of the most elegant catering restaurants in New Jersey. In fact, we were the first school from Newark to have our prom there, the West Orange Manor. What a swanky place. We pulled up to the door and all of the kids were gathered at the door waiting to go in for pictures. The limo driver got out and came around to the door and opened it. The kids standing there were the jocks and cheerleaders, all of the elite of our class with their dates. When they saw two nobodies from school get out of a limo being driven by a white chauffeur and he opened the door for us, their mouths dropped to the floor in shock. They just stared at us in a jealous way.

We just walked in with our date as if we were Rockefellers. We took pictures and stayed for a little while and left them there and went to New York. We found the Hawaii Kai club and drank some kind of drinks that had just enough alcohol to feel it. From there, we went to the African Room, from there to another club. Now the night was getting short and we had to get our dates home. We got in around 3:00 a.m.

My dad said, "Wow, boy, you must have had a good time."

I said, "Yes, I did." Knowing what he was thinking about what I had done with Gracie, but that didn't happen, it didn't come up at all, I respected her too much and we had already talked about marriage even at this young age. Yes, *marriage*. So graduation came in a few weeks after the prom and we hired the same limo company with the same driver. He called us good kids and he asked for us. After graduation, I found a traveling salesmen job, just to get away from my dad, even though he never laid hands on me ever again, I still wanted to get away from his drinking and antics.

Now that I look back and understand, my father suffered from P.T.S.D. from being in the war in Korea. Graduation was a milestone for me. School was not my strong suit. My goal was to go into the Navy, and before this traveling salesmen job came up, I'd gone to the Navy recruiting station, and they told me that they couldn't take me because I was only seventeen. I was so disappointed. I left the Navy recruiting station and, in a few days, I went to the Air Force recruiter and they allowed me to take the written test. The results came back in a few days. The recruiter called and said that I passed and scored high in electronics. Wow, this was good news to me. So he told me that I should come back for the physical. So in a few days, I went down to the federal building to take the physical. After the exam, one of the doctors asked me if I had taken PT in high school. Of course I said *yes*, and I had taken all three years of gym. The reason he asked me this is because he said that I had a heart murmur. This was news to me. He said if you can get a letter from the board of education showing my record of gym, they would accept me. So I went there and requested the letter then returned. Even though the letter was clear, they decided not to admit me into the Air Force.

Well, you can only imagine how I felt. This had been my life's dream to go into the military. So from that point, I started looking for other methods of escape. So one day, I was looking in the want ads of the Newark Star Ledger newspaper and there it was, a traveling sales job. Wow, just what I'm looking for. It's summer of 1968 and now I don't want to leave my Gracie, but she understood what I was going through at home. So I told her that I would come home on the weekends.

I went to the hotel where the interviews were being held and, because of how I dressed with shirt and a tie, they hired me. They told me to go pack a bag and meet them back here at the Holiday Inn. I ran home, got there before my father and packed a suitcase. On my way out the door, he came in and asked where I was going. I told him that I had gotten a job traveling around the east coast selling magazine subscriptions. He reluctantly agreed. I said *so long* to Gracie and departed.

We went down to Camden, N.J. and started going from door to door, telling people that we were working our way through college and they bought it. Man, I was good at getting people to write those checks. After a week or so, I wondered when I was going to get paid. I ask the handler and he said that they hold our pay for hotel payments of our rooms and food vouchers for the restaurants. So I accepted that and continued working. Now there were both girls and boys on the road together. At night after we finished work, we would go to the restaurant to eat. Then, we were in Pennsylvania working and the weekend came. I remembered what I'd told Gracie and I wanted to go see her but had no way of getting back to Jersey, so I called her. She was upset that I couldn't come home. In the meantime, I was fooling around with these girls on the team.

Before I knew it, the month of September came in and I'd been made one of the drivers, dropping the other kids off in different neighborhoods and going back to pick them up. By then, I knew that this was a scam. I didn't have a driver's license, just a permit from high school. I had told the manager that I was twenty-three and he believed me. So here I was driving in Maryland, Washington D.C. and Virginia with no license. I had control of a 1967 Chevy Impala; I thought I was King Tut.

But something was wrong at home. My girl didn't sound so happy to hear my lie about coming home for the weekend. I told my manager that I need my money to go home for the weekend, he told me that I could take the car and go and come back. I thought about it for a minute and decided not to take him up on that idea. He gave me some money and I departed on the bus out of Washington D.C. and went home. The first week of October, I arrived home. I'd been away since August. I called up Gracie and told her that I was home. She didn't respond the way that I thought she would. So I asked her if I could come to see her and she said *yes*. I went up to her house and we talked, but she was distant to me and I questioned her love for me. She explained that while I was gone, her aunt tried to get her to date other boys and she refused. She said that I was coming home for the weekend, but I didn't show up. She didn't go out with anyone while I was away, so I didn't go back to that job. After a few days, the manager called the house and asked my dad why I didn't return. He also told my dad what I was doing and that I was one of his best drivers.

My dad said, "Driver? He doesn't have a license."

The manager also told my dad that I'd claimed that I was twenty-three. Of course, my dad told him that I was only seventeen. So I explained to my father that, yes, I'd told that untruth. He just shook it off and walked away. However, things with Gracie got a lot better and I found another Job in Kearny, N.J. at Celutone Plastics. I worked and forgot all about going anywhere else.

Christmas of 1968 came and I decided that I would make a visit to my home town. So I told Gracie this and she said, "Don't stay too long."

I took the bus down to Louisiana. I went to my Grammo's house and she was overwhelmed to see me and was amazed at how I had grown up in two and a half years. I visited all of my relatives.

This was during the time of the civil rights movement and the Jim Crow laws had been lifted in my home town. This was a big shock to me. We went to the movies one night and sat in the downstairs part of the movies. *What a change in the few years since I had been gone.* All of my old friends wanted to know all about New Jersey, and of course, I laid it on thick. What really intrigued them the most was my clothes; they had never seen such fashions.

While at the movies on our way in I see the girl that I told you about earlier in my story. Her mouth dropped and she was happy to see me, but now I was taller than the last time she saw me, and dressed to the nines. That was a good feeling. I said *hello* and walked away like I had seen James Bond perform in the movies. Soon, it was time to go home, back to my Gracie.

My Grammo was surprised that I came back after the way that I had left and all of the negativity that I experienced there. But all of that was behind me now and I didn't dwell on the past. After a few days, I was on the bus going back home. I called Gracie and told her that I was coming home.

New Year's Day came and we spent the day together. As time went on, Gracie and I became closer and closer. I knew that this girl was my future wife and we talked about it a lot. Now by this time, I had given up on going into the military, so I went to work every day and back home in the evening. I didn't make a lot of money at Celutone Plastics, but I learned more about being an adult with the responsibility of taking care of myself, buying clothes and taking my girl to nice places. Always a gentleman, opening doors for her and frequently going to nice restaurants like Momma Leonia's in Manhattan and other fine restaurants.

During the month of February, on a Saturday morning, the phone rang and it was my oldest sister, Donnell. She said that she had gotten a nanny's job in N.Y and wanted to come visit me in Newark. Well this was a huge surprise because I had not seen her since she had gotten married in 1964 or '65 and left Louisiana for Chicago. So, of course, I asked my dad if that could be possible and he said *yes*.

So she took the bus from N.Y. and arrived in Newark. I was looking out the window and spotted her getting off of the bus. I went to meet her, and she was so surprised to see how I had grown up. She stayed a long time talking and of course, my father had the chance to ask about my mother. I hadn't heard from her since she'd left Louisiana in 1965. Donnell talked very little about her in front of present company. So after she went back to N.Y., one day I get a call from her saying the job wasn't working out and she asked if she could come stay with us until she could get a job.

During those days, jobs in Newark were plentiful, even after the riot. The damage from the riot was only in the Black community and not downtown or the industrial areas of the city. So again, I went to my father with this request. He said, "Well, okay, just until she finds a job." I don't know my stepmother's thoughts on this because it was not discussed in front of me.

Chapter Five

In a couple of days, my sister came and moved in. She found a job right away and started saving her money for an apartment. She knew that I was working and had finished high school, so one day, she approached me and said, "Why we don't get an apartment together?"

Now my eldest sister is five years older than me, which meant that she was twenty-two, so I thought about it and discussed it with my dad. He said these words to me, "Son, I could stop you because you are still a minor, but if that's what you feel you need to do, then go ahead."

So after work, we hit the streets with a newspaper, looking for a furnished apartment. Every one that we looked at was not big enough for her. Two bedrooms were all that we needed but she insisted on three or more. In those days, Newark had family houses with large three and four bedrooms. So we finally found one on So. 11th St., off of Avon Ave. We moved in and began fixing up the place, painting and cleaning the joint.

After we got our income tax checks, she said to me, "Why don't we send for Momma and bring her up here from Memphis?"

Now this was the mother who, at an earlier age, I felt didn't care about me. Thank God I didn't feel any animosity towards her. I said, "Okay, let's do it."

I went down to see Gracie one day before we put the plan into action and stopped by my dad's house for a visit. When I told him of our plan, he didn't say anything at first, but before I left, he privately said these words to me – and I will never forget them. "Son, you don't know your mother, she's going to use you. Think about that."

I didn't like his remarks about my mother, but he was speaking from experience. So she came in March with my siblings and my sister's son, Rod. I looked down the stairs of the three-family building from our third-floor apartment, and saw my mother, with five children in tow. I asked myself, *What I have done? Oh man! I'm used to being a bachelor. I don't need this headache.* So I would stay out as much as possible or at my dad's place. Then came the month of May and the 24th of the month was my birthday. I was turning the big eighteen.

One day I came home from work and there was a letter on the table from Uncle Sam, as we called it during the military draft days. Well, it was from the Army telling me to report to the federal building downtown. I didn't take to that so kindly, because I had heard of how many Army soldiers were getting killed in Viet Nam. So to keep from going to jail, I went downtown to the federal building to enlist. Low and behold, while waiting on the sergeant to come swear us in, a Marine gunnery sergeant came into the room, pointed and said, "You, and you, come with me."

So, I was one of those he'd pointed at. So I was drafted into the Marine Corps. By then, my father was an inpatient at the VA hospital detox clinic. So I went up to give the news of going into the Marines. He didn't take it too well and said, "Boy, you don't know what you have done. The Marines are crazy."

I just shrugged it off and begin to prepare for my exit. The next person I told was my Gracie. She thought that I was kidding, she kind of laughed it off. That was the end of June of 1969. By July fifth, I had to report for transport to Parris Island Boot camp. So July fourth, I spent the day with Gracie telling her about tomorrow's exit from home. At the time she worked for the board of education near the Federal building, on a summer school program. So after reporting to the Gunnery Sgt., he allow me to go say goodbye to my Gracie.

I went over there and she began to cry when I told her that I was leaving for boot camp. We promised to write every day. So along with the other recruits, I boarded the train to South Carolina. Arriving in Bufford S.C., we got on buses to the base. We got there after 10:00 p.m. The bus stopped and, in a few moments, this very large D.I. got on the bus. He looked like someone melted his uniform onto his body. He said some very colorful metaphors and said that we had ten seconds to get off the bus and nine them are gone. Well we ran over each other getting off of the bus and on to the yellow foot prints painted on the ground. They harassed us all night, allowing us to go upstairs and lay on the bunks and then in a few moments coming back, just as we fell asleep. Well, my dad's words begin to resound in my head. I began to cry and I said to myself, *I've been sent to hell.*

Well, boot camp in the Marines in 1969 was just that, hell on earth. After two weeks, I said to myself, I can do this, I'm going to make it and go home with a stripe on my uniform. Ten weeks was the longest of my young life. In August of that time, only a few more weeks and I would graduate. The date was set for September tenth. My Gracie and I wrote weekly and she told me that she was going to visit some relatives in S.C. and that she was going to have them bring her down to boot camp to visit me. Well, this was a big problem in recruit training, but I told her to come on anyway. She arrived and they told her she couldn't see me. She said that she came all the way from N.J. to see me and begin to make a fuss about it. They agreed to let her see me for two hours and that's it.

Headquarters called my barracks and told my D.I. Staff Sgt. Suddith. He called me to the D.I. hut and told me that I had a visitor and he would deal with me when I came back. I didn't care what he would make me do; I was going to see my girl. I ran all the way to main side and there she was. Oh my goodness, she was so beautiful to me, we spent the two hours talking and holding hands. Her cousin, the same one from earlier in this story, was there as well. The time went by so quickly and then she was gone. When I returned back to the barracks, the D.I. was waiting for me. After he called me some names that I can't repeat here in this book, he said get down and give me 100 push ups. By this time in boot camp, I was in the best shape of my young life. I did them with pleasure after seeing my Gracie. Soon graduation day came and off to ITR training in Camp Lejeune, N.C., another three months of training for Viet Nam. Then just before Thanksgiving, we were flown home, my first time on an airplane. In ITR training, we rode on a helicopter but no plane. This was very exciting for me. I had earned that PFC stripe on my uniform and, once again, the prophecy over my own life had come to pass.

Between my youth and no relationship with God, my thought process was instinctual. Arriving home and saying *hello* to my sister Donnell, I dropped my duffel bag and headed out the door in uniform. My sister said that Momma worked in the commercial laundry company up the street from where we lived on So. 11th Street. I stopped in to say *hello* to my mother and she wanted all of her co-workers to know that her son was a Marine. After leaving the laundry, I headed to the bus stop on Springfield Ave., going north to Broom Street.

Gracie was working at the Food Town Supermarket up the street from the projects, so I got off the bus and walked into the supermarket and I can't tell you the excitement in the both of us. We hugged and her boss told her after seeing the excitement that she could go and be with her Marine. I walked her home, a few blocks from the supermarket. Her aunt and uncle greeted me with such joy; we spent the rest of the day together talking of our plans to marry as soon as she graduated from high school in June of 1970. I had money from boot camp. During training, there is no need for recruits to have money, so when going home, you get all of your pay. Wow, in 1969, $480.00 dollars was a lot of money and was the full amount of back pay from boot camp and ITR training. In 1969, that was a nice sum of money!

So for twenty-one days, I took her to the best places on our dates. My dad saw me in my uniform and he had big respect for me. He was so proud of me, making it out of the Marine Corps boot camp alive and well. Again, he also told all of his friends about me being a Marine. In my neighborhood, very few went into the Corps, most guys were drafted into the Army. I saw some of my old friends and we had some good laughs. Now that twenty-one-day leave was coming to an end. I had to return to the Marines. The time came and we spent the last moment together before I flew to California for jungle warfare training for Viet Nam.

I arrived in Los Angeles and took the bus down to Camp Pendleton. We were there a couple of days and I thought to myself that I told my Grammo, that when I reached the age of eighteen, that I would return to California. Again prophecy was fulfilled over my life. Two days later, they formed us up and said that our Battalion was being disbanded and we all were going to be shipped to other bases. When they got to me, they said, "You are going to Quantico."

I said, "Quantico? Where is that?"

The Sgt. said, "It's an officer's training base in Virginia."

My goodness, that's close to Jersey. Good, I was over-joyed with this news. Then, it was back on the plane to the east coast. As soon as we landed, I called Gracie and told her that I was going to be stationed near her in Virginia. She was happy knowing I would come up when I could on the weekends. Quantico was some very good duty. Training Marine Corps Officers. Spit and polish. This was right up my alley. I loved being a Marine and did well on my inspections and gained even more rank as time went by.

June came, and Gracie graduated from high school. Just as we had planned, we were married on the 27th of June, 1970. A corporal friend of mine allowed me to wear his dress blues to get married in. I had a good record with the company XO, and had done well in the Base General's inspection. Actually, I'd done so well that he gave me ten days free leave and a 96-hour pass. That 96-hour pass was for the most outstanding inspection report. I won that pass as well as the ten free days, that's a total of fourteen days to be with my new bride. Even then, God was with me showing me favor, and I didn't even know that He was watching over me. Just to be stationed so close to the nation's capital and so close to home. Now that's favor.

He said in His Word that He would show us favor with mankind. I didn't have a relationship with Him as of yet. But what I had was that touch from my experience on the floor of that little church years earlier in Louisiana. After returning to the base, I applied for base housing and bought my bride down to Virginia. We were given a furnished, three-bedroom bun-galow. The Corps knows how to treat their Marines, even the enlisted men.

We enjoyed our honeymoon in the hotel that the base kept just for newly married Marines. Oh, what joy we had. We were finally allowed to be together as husband and wife. I was only nineteen years old, and she had turned eighteen the previous November. We didn't know what we were doing, but we knew that we loved each other and wanted a life together.

As time went on, I made another rank. However, by November, I received orders to Viet Nam. We'd had three months together at Midway base housing. Now, the reality of being in the armed forces sounded off with a big wake-up call. Again, Gracie and I were being separated. Her uncle came down and took her and our few belongings home to Jersey. A few days afterward, I joined them for a twenty-one-day leave. Nearing Christmas of 1970, I was off to Viet Nam. I landed back at Camp Pendleton for jungle training again. This was a two-week process. In the meantime, I knew that I had relatives in Los Angeles, so I looked them up. I visited my uncles, Pete and Ronald, who were my mother's brothers.

Pete, the oldest brother, was where I went to first. I had not seen him since he'd come back from the Army in 1964. What a change in me he saw. We spent hours laughing and talking about when I was a kid. Ronald was my next stop, and like with Pete, we bonded again. It was quite an experience seeing my family again, along with cousins – their children. The two weeks went pretty fast and the next thing I knew, I was on a journey towards Viet Nam.

The Marine Corps don't tell you that you're going over there. They tell you that you are going to Okinawa, Japan. After a fourteen-hour flight from Hawaii, we landed in Japan. We were bused to our units, and deep down inside, I felt that I would continue to Nam. The Marines that I'd gone through jungle training with began unpacking their duffel bags and putting their uniforms in the cleaners. I never unpacked, and sure enough, they told me where I was going.

Now, with Viet Nam a reality in my near future, I felt fear and didn't know what to expect. We went to a big warehouse and got jungle battle dress uniforms; I knew this was actually happening. The next day, we boarded a commercial airline, Braniff International Airlines. We headed to Nam, a 3,000 mile Journey. I thought bombs would be exploding on the airstrip where we were going to land, but no bombs at all. This was Da Nang Viet Nam Marine Corps Headquarters.

Soon after arriving, we were shipped out to FireBase Baldy, a heavily defended firebase. From there, we went directly to the bush. I was a non-commissioned officer, E-4. Yet, because I was green to combat, I was put at the rear of the squad on long patrols. I was called tail-end-Charlie. I walked backward a lot of the time, looking for *Charlie* as the Vietnamese were called. We called them some other names. I saw some pretty awful things on my tour of the war. There are things that I still suffer P.T.S.D. from, even to this day.

Thank God for help and His divine protection over there. I spent only three months in that war but saw action the whole time being there. My MOS was 0311, a rifleman, Combat Marine. The reason I spent only three months was because when I went there, I only had six months left on my enlistment. I came home after 'Nam different than before I went. We would be in the bush for thirty days at a time, coming back to Baldy and R&R for a couple of days, then back to the bush.

It was a terrifying experience, to say the least. After about a week, the Red Cross notified my wife that I was in Viet Nam and gave her the address to write to me, and she did. In her package she sent to me was some junk food and underwear, but they were white. All of my buddies laughed and said that she was trying to collect on my policy. She just didn't know any better. White underwear was the last thing I needed in a warzone. Allow me to elaborate, in jungle warfare, or any combat fighting, a Marine with a white tee shirt on would be a clear target for a sniper's round!

My aunt sent me a care package, as well. In the box was a small can of peaches, pudding, and chocolate cakes that was a mound of crumbs and chocolate icing. My fellow marine buddies and I gathered around and ate every bit of the cake crumbs. The next day, it was time for my squad to go out on patrol. This was an L.R.R.P. – long-range recon patrol. It was my first time in that country.

Of course, I was aware of my fear. We went down the mountain into Antenna Valley. The reason it was named this was because of the high elephant grass, that sometimes would reach high into the air, up to six or seven feet high. This would cause the radioman to put on the twelve-foot antenna to reach our rear in case we needed support. The enemy would target the twelve-foot antenna and kill the radioman. This didn't happen on this patrol. We didn't encounter any NVA or Viet Cong troops. Afterward, we returned to our area of observation, better known as our AO. On our ascent of the mountain, we received machine-gun fire from above us, at the midway point of the ascent.

We all hit the deck and started firing in the direction of the incoming rounds, only to find out it was friendly fire coming from a helicopter Evac team above us. We stopped our return fire after the Lt. radioed the chopper pilots and said, "Cease fire, cease fire!"

Wow, you see your life come in front of you in slow motion when death is possible. I thought that I could melt into the ground because I was lying that flat on it. We had a big story to tell our buddies when we arrived back at the AO.

The next day I received a letter from my wife telling me that she was pregnant with our first child. Before we left Quantico, she had conceived our child. Oh boy, what rejoicing I did with my fellow Marine buddies. You see, the Marine Corps taught us in boot camp about camaraderie. We had a bond and had each other's back, both in combat situations and against any other intruders.

That night we huddled in a fighting hole and, for the first time in Nam, I was offered a joint. At first, I was hesitant to try it, and of course, I was coached by the buddies. Man, what a feeling that was. That started my drug use in Nam that I later carried home. Even then, my God didn't allow one scratch to come upon me. After many patrols and some firefights, we return to the rear at FireBase Baldy. In the rear, we would of course, hide away and do drugs and drink beer, which was not my favorite. After being in the rear for two days, we were told that we had to provide protection to the local village.

Viet Cong would go into the villages of the Vietnamese, people that they thought were friendly toward us. They would kill the leaders of the village and anyone else that they thought was a threat to their movement toward communist. We did our job that night. In a few days, it was back to the bush. After thirty days out there, we were called back to the rear for a big, full Battalion operation into enemy territory. Now it was my job to drop concussion grenades into tunnels that the VC had dug.

I went through the area doing this, and the Lt. said, "Hey, baby wings, if those were frags, you would be dead. Throw them in and move out from the area."

This was my first time with this assignment. So from that point on, I did as I was commanded by Lt. This was my first experience seeing dead VC. It wasn't a pleasant experience. I'm telling this story about my experience in the war to show God's protection of me, His soon-to-be servant. I did not sustain one physical scratch, but mental damage was another story. After the operation, we returned back to the area that we had been in before, and we stayed and patrolled the area daily. Then we were given moving orders, so we began packing up to move to a new location.

While waiting on the choppers, we looked out into the valley and saw the fog moving in. This was monsoon season and it rained every day like clockwork. Before packing our gear, we had to eliminate canned foods because of the weight limits on the choppers. The practice was to punch holes in the cans and bury them with booby traps, such as CS grenades. After five days with no solid food, we ate only candy bars and crackers that some Marines had in their rock packs. Drinking water came from the waterfall. We decided to dig up some cans and carefully dismantle the booby traps. After five days, the worms had entered the cans; however, we made a fire and dumped everything into a helmet, with hot sauce, salt, pepper, and ketchup, We also cooked the worms.

So the reason that I mention this is to assure my readers that you can never say what you are not willing to eat to survive. After two more days, the fog lifted and by this time, we were lifted back to the 7up pad on Baldy. The supply hooch was there near the 7up pad and the Lt. said that we could jump the fence and get apples and other fruit, not knowing that Battalion had left the Chow hall open for us with steak and potatoes waiting. Wow, what a feast! Unaware to me, this would be my last experience in Viet Nam. A week later, we were on our way back to the Big PX, as we called *home*. We were checked medically for physical damages and inspected for shaves and haircuts. Back to Da Nang for transport back to Okinawa.

When we arrived there, we had two days before our flight home, so I went to the tailor's shop that I heard about from other Marines and had a suit made from my measurements. What a fit. The tailor told me to come back in the morning and my suit would be ready. Sure enough, I went the next day and there it was, my first custom suit. It fit so well, and because I love clothes, I was extremely proud of my first custom-made suit. In 'Nam, we used MPC for purchasing things. That's military paper currency. It looked like monopoly money. But now we had cash from our back pay.

The next day we boarded flights back home, landing at Travis Air Force Base and transported to Camp Pendleton. What amazed me about returning home was all of the lights. Being in pitch black darkness at night, except for the flares that went up, or the moonlight in 'Nam, there weren't any lights in the bush.

I am reminded of an event that I experienced in the Nam. We had a night patrol called a KT; it stands for Killer Team patrol. Four Marines were heavily armed with an M60 Machine gun, with lots of ammunition, fragmentation grenades, and a weapon called by Marines, a blooper, which was a grenade launcher. Four men set up an ambush for Charlie.

This was a terrifying experience. Mosquitoes were the size of a drone aircraft attacking you. Very large scorpions and snakes were really dangerous – one bite will end your life. This is some of what we had to contend with in 'Nam.

Chapter Six

I WANT YOU TO KNOW just some of the life-ending events that the Lord saved me from in The 'Nam. Not knowing of His divine protection, all I can remember was praying to get home to my wife and unborn child. When we arrived at the base, they put us up in a barracks until morning. The next day we received our mustering out physical and final pay. I got in touch with my uncle Pete and went to LA, California. When I arrived, he had a little party for me, and by then, I was a full weed head, smoking all of the marijuana that came my way. It was the habit that I brought back home with me.

My uncle said to me, "Duke, don't go home to your wife, stay here and send for her. I will get you on at General Motors with Ronald and me. But if you go home, you won't come back."

I wanted to see my wife right away, so I didn't listen. He didn't mention it again. The next day I caught a flight to Newark, N.J. Arriving after a long flight, I took a taxi home to the projects and my Gracie. What a reunion. By now, she was showing a little with our child. The first thing I did was go back to my old job, Celutone Plastics. What a boring job. I had matured to adulthood and, after the military, this job didn't cut it anymore. I was married with a child on the way and we need our own place. So we found a two-bedroom apartment on So. 19th Street in Newark. We applied for furniture on credit. *A three-room outfit*, it was called. Living room, dinette set, and a bedroom set, all for around $900.00 plus high finance charges.

We moved in, the furniture was delivered and we started our lives together. This was April 1971. I came home to a new wife. At the time of my first child's birth, I was getting high on weed and drinking. I spent a lot of time going to bars and hanging out with friends. However, my wife was getting more involved with church activities and living a Christian life. I didn't want any part of church, but didn't stop her from going. This only allowed me to do what I wanted while she was gone. Unaware to me, she had the church praying for me. The time for my baby to be born came and it was the hospital's policy not to let the father into the delivery room to observe the birth, so I went to a bar and was drinking, waiting on a phone call to the phone booth in the bar.

The phone rang and the nurse said that I had a beautiful baby girl, six pounds and some ounces. I was very happy and rushed up to the hospital. There my wife and our new baby girl was lying in her arms. She was so beautiful, looking like both of us, so small and tiny. I was afraid to hold her. When I brought them home, I would hold her and allow her to fall asleep on my chest. She became really attached to me and I to her. This was my little baby doll. All of the family adored our little baby doll, and my mother would babysit her while Gracie and I worked. What a joy she brought into our lives.

While I had been away in the 'Nam, my wife gave her life to the Lord. She was saved through my mother, who had also been reclaimed after backsliding when she came to Newark in 1969. Now this was a whole new problem for me, I didn't want any part of going to the church. While my wife was attending church on Sunday with my mother and oldest sister, I was home getting high. I didn't want her to know of my habit so I would spray air refresher and burn incense. When she would arrive home I was well lit up. She noticed the change in me. Walter was not the same Walter that he was when he left home. She didn't brow beat me about going to church with her but every now and then I would go. I didn't like the service; I felt that the preacher talked too long and that he was talking to me.

In the church, there was a minister named Elder Henry Pringle. I learned that he had a construction business and he liked my mother. Well, I figured that this was a way of getting a better job. I would go to church and put up with getting out of church around 3:00 p.m. from an 11:30 a.m. start. Wow, those old Pentecostal preachers were very long-winded. So I approached him about work. He gladly said, *yes,* that I could come work with him.

So I left Celutone Plastics and began working for him. Oh my goodness, what back-breaking work. Mixing cement, setting up scaffolding, I did any other odd jobs on the job site. What I didn't realize, was that God was at work through him. I smoked cigarettes as well and I knew this didn't sit well with Pentecostal preachers, so I would quit for a day or two while around the job site. One day he inquired about my mother. I said to myself, *Oh so that's it.* He wants to date my mother. She was a very beautiful woman, and he would ask questions about her and I would relay them to my sister.

The next thing I knew was that Grace and I had tickets to a banquet downtown at the Holiday Inn hotel with, *guess who?* Elder Pringle and my mother. So I guess I played a part in them getting together, because in a few months they were married. I stood and gave my mother away to him in marriage. That was an honor. I was very happy for my mother and my siblings. He gave Jesse and Kenneth his last name through adoption. This kind of gave me an insight into the class of man that he was. That he would take a woman with four children and marry her was a sign of a good man.

As I worked with him, I realized that he is a true man of God, just by his speech and interactions with his employees. So I developed a very high respect for him. Still doing my thing at home and with friends on occasions. As the hot weather came in, I was working in the hot sun, mixing cement and building scaffolding. It was very hard work. We would arrive at the job site at dawn and work until 4:00 or 5:00 o'clock in the evening. I'd come home worn out. So, after about six months on the job, I decided on one rainy day to go down to the VA to talk to a counselor about employment. At that time, the VA had a few jobs for vets coming back from 'Nam. I met with a counselor and he found three jobs on microfilm. The first was working for an advertising company in New York, and the second was learning the silversmith trade as an apprentice, or the Penn Central Railroad. You guessed it. I took the railroad interview. They wanted to give jobs to 'Nam vets.

Going over to New York Penn Station, I met with the company interviewer and he said that I had to take an exam to qualify for this position. The room was full of young men like me. Now that concerned me because I'd been just a C student in high school. So they gave us the test, the first part was true or false questions and multiple choice; it wasn't as bad as I'd thought.

When we were almost finished, after about three hours, they said to us, "If we tell you to come back tomorrow for the second half of the test, that means that you passed the first part."

At the end of the day, I was one of the persons who were told to come back. Here again, God's favor was upon me and I didn't even realize it. The next day we returned and it was not even half of the first group. I felt so lucky, but it wasn't luck that got me that far. It was God's favor upon my young life. The second half of the test was all mechanical and some electrical. I passed the second half of the test and was told with a group of other young men to report tomorrow for a physical exam, which all of us passed. The next few days consisted of classes and field trips on the trains. Then they sent us to trainman school in Philadelphia for three days to learn the rail rules and track signals. I loved the classes and learned how to do my job.

When we got back to New York, they said that I would be going into freight service, but before leaving, the powers-that-be said, *You're going into passenger service.* This meant more classes on ticket collection, fare beaters, and the different lines of service between New York and Philadelphia. Great, this meant that I would also wear a snappy conductor's uniform. I wore a dark blue jacket, white shirt and black tie, with the conductor's hat. I loved uniforms anyway, from being a Marine. So I started working and making a lot of money. But I realized something. I never mentioned my exit from my old job. I didn't do it right. I just stopped going to work, no call, no two-weeks' notice to my stepdad, I just quit.

These are some of the characteristics of youth. I was only twenty-one years old and didn't realize the importance of having good moral values. But this man of God didn't hold it against me. Because I had to report to different rail yards to pick up trains, I needed a car. Believe it or not, through God, He helped me to get my first car. It was a 1967 Thunderbird – green with a tan leather interior. What a beautiful car. I would now be able to take on-call jobs at a moment's notice. Sometimes, they would call at 4:00 a.m. and say that I had a train in the county yard, in New Brunswick. I was to bring it up to New York.

With the new job, I was making so much money, but I was still partying every weekend while my wife and daughter whom I affectionately call *baby doll*, was over a year old and walking, went to church on Sunday. After a while, I started picking up women on the train and not going straight home after my shift. One day, I met a friend on the railroad. He had a sister whose boyfriend was a big coke dealer. We would go over to their house when her boyfriend wasn't home and sniff a lot of his product. Eventually, this lifestyle led me to start dipping into railroad money, which led to a lot of problems.

Taking money was one of the forbidden rules of the railroad. We had forty-eight hours after a round trip shift that took us to Washington D.C. then back to New York. That shift was great money – on top of what our regular shift work would pay. It paid a bonus of $125.00 for the one-way trip, plus *deadhead* pay, coming back at so much a mile. Deadheading was a term used to Identify trainmen that were just riding the train back to their originating station, not working the train back. A lot of times they would ask us to work the train back up to New York, that was another $125.00 plus mileage. Total we would collect around $350.00 for an overnight trip. This was 1972. You see how much of a blessing this job was.

One day, I took a freight job to Harrisburg, Pennsylvania after not turning the money in as I should. The money collected from a previous trip had to be turned in within forty-eight hours, or that conductor had to have a really good reason for not doing so. This had been more than the allotted time.

On the way back, dispatch told the train engineer to have me report tomorrow to the union office for a hearing. I was sweating bullets. I reported and was told to either resign or be fired – my only choices. I left that day with my head down, knowing that I had blown the best job that I could have ever had.

I went home and told my wife that I was fired. She consoled me and said that I would find something else. Well, I didn't really look for anything else. I was so embarrassed to tell anyone that I had lost my railroad job after only six months on the job.

So I decided that I needed a fresh start out of Jersey, so I went to the Marine recruiter and re-enlisted back into the corps. I have been out a year and nine months. They gave me E-2, which is PFC. When I'd gotten out, I'd been an E-4. I lost two stripes. It didn't matter. After resigning from the railroad in late September, I didn't look for another job, because of my heart-felt loss of the best job that I could ever have. I started drinking more and getting high on weed and cocaine.

I began to think about my actions and realized that something had to change. One day, my brother Donald called and said that he was coming to New Jersey. I had not seen him since his dad came and took him back to Texas. Oh, wow, my brother was coming. After arriving in Newark, I found out that he had the same habits as I did. He moved in with Momma and Pop. Soon after he was there, I had re-enlisted back into the Marines, just for a fresh start. I told Gracie that we need a fresh start, and California was where we would start. I knew in my heart that if we stayed in Jersey, things would only get worse. I told my wife that we were going to Camp Pendleton in California. I knew in my heart that if we stayed in Jersey, things would only get worse. She agreed and we sold all of our furniture, and I turned the car back into the finance company. They weren't too happy about that. I got permission from Gracie's uncle for her to stay there until I get settled in my new base. He agreed. But her two oldest sisters didn't like the idea of me taking their little sister so far from home. I didn't care about that. She's my wife and this is what I thought would make me a better person and a better provider. I left Newark in November and came back after

Christmas to get Gracie and my little Baby Doll. I had found our first apartment in San Clemente California. Rent was $105.00 a month for a one-bedroom apartment right off of the main drag, El Comino Real.

The Captain that re-enlisted me promised me a lateral move out of the 0311 infantry field and into the 4900 field. This was audiovisual equipment operations. So when I got to California, I was put into 3/7, an infantry battalion. They said it would be temporary until my orders arrived from 8th and I in Washington, D.C. So I settled in and was assigned to a platoon. After getting new uniforms and equipment, I started doing everything the young troops did. The running just about killed me. Now I was a smoker and it took a toll on me. I took leave to go get my family and bring them out here. Our daughter, Quanika, was now a toddler, going on two. So I made the journey back to Jersey to get them. My wife's sisters were still very upset with me, taking their baby sister all the way to California. Before leaving, we sold all of our furniture and gave a lot of things away. It was my thought never to live in Jersey again. However, our destinies were already planned out by God!

Arriving back in California with Gracie and Quanika in tow, we went to my sister Dorothy's apartment. She and Donald had only been married a few months. We stayed overnight with them, leaving some items to collect later on. My stereo component and T.V. were left and when we came back, Donald tried to talk me into leaving it with him a little longer, however I said, "No," with vigor. This was the age of new beginnings in the sound and technology field. He had never heard such sound coming from a component set before, and he tried to keep it for a little while longer. Leaving Los Angeles, we settled in and I reported back to base. I would check weekly about my transfer out of the unit. One day, I asked the SSgt in the office to see my

SRB, that's Service Record Book. He hesitated and reluctantly gave it to me. When I looked where my lateral move forms were, the forms weren't there. They should have been in there. They were all missing except one page. So I questioned the Sgt. about it and naturally, he denied knowing anything about it.

I went back to my unit and the other Black Marines told me that, in that office, there is a lot of racism. With that, I knew that I had an enemy in the office. Every other week I would go up and ask about my lateral move. So after about three months there, the battalion was prepping for cold weather training in Nevada. This was a thirty-day training operation – I didn't want to go on and leave my family in town by themselves. A Gunnery Sgt. from another unit seemed to take a liking to me.

He said, "Dukes, I'm going to tell you how to solve your problem, but you didn't hear this from me. You can't jump the chain of command without being court marshaled, but your wife can. Have her call the base General's office and tell them of your dilemma."

Well, the next day she did just that, telling the General's staff all about the promise of my lateral move by the Captain who took me in. There is a saying in the military, *stuff rolls downhill.* The General called Regiment, Regiment called Battalion, Battalion called the Company Commander. He sent for Lance Corporal Dukes. He walked up one side of me and down the other, but all that I could do at the moment was stand still at attention

This prevented me from going to Nevada for cold weather training, however I did get punished for my dastardly deed. One part of the papers for my lateral move was left in my SRB so they had to honor the promise. The Captain told me that it had to wait until they got back from Nevada.

"Dukes, you are going on guard duty while we are away. Get out of my office and report back to your Platoon," he said.

The Platoon LT. sent me to the guard unit. This meant four hours on, four hours off – during the night – and twelve hours off during the day. So I went home and told Gracie of my new schedule.

She asked, "Well, why don't I go home for the thirty days?"

I sent her and our baby girl back to Jersey. Up until three months of my re-enlistment, I hitched to work every day. Marines would pick up other Marines hitching along the road each morning. About this time I had bought a 1969 Pontiac Firebird – oh, what a fast car. The Firebird color was Champagne Green with the interior a little darker green. I would give other Marines rides back and forth to the base for guard duty and drop them off back after our twelve-hour shifts.

One day after Gracie and the baby were back home, I was coming home and a Marine who was being discharged on a Bad Conduct Discharge crashed into the back of my car and totaled it. Just like that, I was without a car again because he didn't have insurance and I only had liability. So my transfer came to Main side where the film library was located, this was twenty miles from San Clemente, I was back to hitching again.

But, I had a neighbor who also was a Marine. He said, "Don't sweat it. I will sell you my car for $400.00." It was a 1967 Nova SS 327 engine and four-speed Mumsie shifter.

I've got wheels again! I reported to the Base Film Library for duty as an Audio Visual Equipment operator. What I didn't realize was that the company commander had put in my SRB by code that I was a trouble maker and non-comp, which meant that my new assignment would not receive me too nicely. Of course, the Master Sgt. E-8 gave me all of the worst jobs that he could think of, like cutting up old World War II training films.

This didn't matter to me because I wasn't going into the field on Infantry ops.

I'd be home every night with my family. One day, the Master Sgt. called me into his office for some harassment and said, "You are going on Mess Duty."

That meant getting up at 3:00 a.m. to be to the Mess Hall by 4:30 a.m. When I would leave home and go through the base to get to the Main side, the fog would be so thick that I couldn't see the road and, on base, there were mountains with no guardrails in some places. Carefully and slowly, I would drive the twenty miles. By then, Grace was pregnant with our second child. Two pregnancies with her malfunctioning heart.

Then, the Master Sgt. told me that I had to stay in the Barracks with the other Marines during Mess Hall duty. I told him that my wife was expecting our second child and had a bad heart. He said that was my problem and not the Marine Corps. Well, he didn't know this old salty Marine. I accepted his orders, then had Gracie call the Commander of the Film Library to complain and tell of our dilemma.

One call to my Master Sgt. and I was off mess duty by the third or fourth day. Then came the retaliation. After about two weeks, they called me into the office and said that I was being transferred to Schools Battalion as an operator in the T.V. studio. This was a cake job, home every evening and all I did was operate Beta Max video recorders and cameras for troops coming up for classes in their MOS out of San Diego boot camp. When the day was over, I went home to Gracie and my baby girl.

One day before leaving the film library, I got a call that it was time for the delivery of our next baby. I got in that Nova and was speeding through the base, breaking all the speed limits. An MP stopped me and asked where I was going so fast. I told him my wife's water had broken and I had to get to San Clemente immediately. So he gave me an escort through the base – going really fast. I enjoyed that.

Gracie didn't like that car because it had loud mufflers and went too fast for her but that day she rode with no complaints. She gave birth to our second child, Ishia Cecilia, named after my mother and one of my favorite aunts. We moved onto base shortly after that so I wouldn't have to make the twenty-mile journey to base – plus base housing was more affordable. I had a few part-time jobs to make ends meet. I worked in a hot laundry. Also, I worked at a dinner as a dishwasher at night. Then as we were settling in to our new base housing, I was promoted to E-4.

They built a new Staff NCO club with a very modern restaurant and night club not far from Wire Mountain where the base housing units were, so I got a job as a waiter and worked there at night. I reverted to the same old Walter, meeting people that I shouldn't be with after work, not going home. One morning, I came home after a night out, and Gracie was tired of my antics. She took my car and left. Gracie didn't have a driver's license. I panicked because I had to report for duty. She made it where ever she went and came back. I jumped in the car and sped off. That evening, when I arrived home, she was still hot and we had a discussion. From that time on, I didn't stay out all night anymore.

Soon my job changed again. I became the company PMI, that's the instructor on the firing range. They gave me this job because the studio was closing down. The troops were being trained down on the Recruit Depot. My rifle score on the range was *expert* so they gave me the job of PMI. I liked this job because of the distance from the brass at headquarters buildings. Before I left the studio, I met an Electrical Engineer who recognized something in me that I didn't know existed. One day as he was working on the patch panel, that was the components that powered all of the equipment for the studio, he said, "Why don't you put your skills to work?"

I said, "What skills?"

He said, "Would you consider building a heathkit?"

"What's a heathkit?"

He pulled out a catalog and showed me a four-channel stereo receiver. I looked at the pictures and said, "I don't think I can do that."

He said, "I believe you can just try it, it comes with all the instructions and they are easy."

So I ordered it and one day, coming home from the rifle range, there was the box, sitting on the floor. Gracie asked what it was.

"A heathkit," I replied.

"What does it cost?"

Well, I didn't want to tell her. But I told her it will keep me busy at home so she was all for it. When I opened the box and saw all those circuit boards and electrical components to be soldered in, I thought *What I have got myself into again?* But, as I began to read the instructions, my thoughts turned to, *Hey, I can do this.* One step at a time. One board at a time. Every day, when I'd get home, I would play a little while with my girls and then straight to the table to work on this kit. By then, I'd quit the waiter job because it kept me in trouble with my wife. Every night home and busy.

Thank God for the engineer! God has a way of helping us out of trouble even when we don't have a relationship with Him. My enlistment was coming to an end and I didn't know what I was going to do. My promotion to E-5 was coming up, but at the same time of my enlistment. Tow years had come to an end.

I talked it over with Gracie and she was really ready to go back to Jersey because there was non of her family in California.

My family is here, I implored her as much as I could, but she still wanted to go home to Jersey. I still didn't want to, so I suggested that she go and see if there were any jobs. This was 1974 during the oil embargo. Gracie was a wise young woman and she knew not to leave me in California alone. She said *no way.* We are going together. So November came and my enlistment ended. The Marine Corps sent movers to pack up our things and we packed up sandwiches and drinks for the 3,000 mile journey to Jersey.

By this time, the Nova had broken down on me and I traded it in for a 1969 Ford Torino. The Ford was more of a family car. After saying goodbye to our friends in the base housing complex, we hit the road at 6:00 a.m. the next morning. We took Interstate 15 through California, Nevada, Arizona, and on to Utah. I drove twelve hours every day and stopped for dinner at night then a hotel. The next day we traveled through Utah and Colorado. The trip was fine until we reached Kansas, then it was boring from there until Jersey. Going through the last states was very tiring, there was very little scenery to look at so it was monotonous.

Then, on the fourth day, we arrived in Newark, New Jersey. As soon as we left the turnpike and entered the city, we hit some major potholes and I started complaining about the streets. Every street in the city was riddled with potholes. I was used to smooth streets in California. We went to my mother's house and they were so happy to see us, especially Ishia, because she looks so much like my mother. They accepted us in to their home and we stayed for about three weeks.

We found jobs right away and found our own apartment. Gracie and I were very independent and we were so used to relying on each other, we dealt with our problems without including family and friends in our personal business. I believe that's the reason our marriage lasted so long. We found an apartment on Elizabeth Ave., in the Weequahic section of Newark. I complained about the city and its inhabitants for six years.

The first job I found was working at The National State Bank as a computer tape librarian, not making a lot of money but employed while going during the day to Dental Tech School. I didn't like the school; I didn't care to be indoors at all. So one day, I was looking in the back of the local newspaper where all of the technical schools advertised, and saw an ad for Pest Management School and job possibilities. So I went to check it out, and after the interview, I liked what I'd heard and seen in the classroom. I started the next week. The professor said that I was doing very well in this field. We would go to classes in the morning and the field in the afternoon. I applied myself to this field and fell in love with entomology. I graduated third highest out of eighty-five students.

Western Termite and Pest Control hired me as a commercial technician. I liked being out on the road every day and interacting with the customers, hospitals, schools, restaurants, and large apartment complexes. After a while, they would have me work on Saturdays with the residential techs. So this broadened my skills.

Then one day the Carpenter Ant tech quit, and the company put me in his place. They sent me back to school for further training in different types of home structures. I learned quickly and was promoted to Carpenter Ant trouble-shooter, handling all company callbacks. I was very good at finding the colony living in the voids of the homes that had already been treated by other techs. Soon I was going into all of the high-end residential communities in New Jersey.

At first, some of the customers didn't like the fact that a Black tech was entering their home. A few went further. They called the office and asked the supervisor why had he sent a "N….." into their home.

Chapter Seven

WELL, THOSE BIGOTED REMARKS didn't make me feel too good, but then, I'd already had plenty of experience with racism while in Louisiana. This just made me work harder to be better than the other technicians. And soon, those same customers were asking that the company send *only me* to solve problems at their homes. I finally found something that I was good at and liked very much.

I went to work every day looking to solve someone's pest problem. As time went by, the company wanted me to work with one of the top managers to develop a system of introducing air pressure to deliver the products into the voids of homes that were being treated. This would enable us to reduce excessive drilling that introduced powders into the homes' walls. So I worked with Gary Jandroph to develop an air pressure system. He was a pleasure to work with. He took my expert opinion on the treatments and we started using this system for pest control and got very good results.

I would work on Saturdays to increase my take-home pay. Soon, we moved from Elizabeth Avenue to Smith Street in the Vailsburg section of Newark near the East Orange border. It was a diverse community of Italian, Hispanic, and Black, which was a very good blend for my family. We were used to living in a diverse community while in California.

In 1976, and my girls were getting bigger. The apartment we'd taken was the first floor of a two-family house. There were two bedrooms, a living room, and dining room – which we'd made our bedroom, and a sunroom in front of the living room. What we didn't know was that the house had to be sanitized from the last tenants. I painted every night when I got home from work and Gracie cleaned, however, we both contracted Hepatitis B; this really made me feel tired and lethargic. I would go jogging and couldn't make my run without stopping. I knew something was wrong, because of the color of my urine. I went to the VA hospital and they quarantined me for twelve days, but it was too late for Gracie. She contracted Hepatitis B. and was hospitalized just as I was being released. I thank God that the children didn't contract it.

We sent the girls to Gracie's aunt's house until we were released from hospital. I lost a lot of weight after this ordeal and looked sick. I recovered and went back to work, so did Grace. Now, this was the beginning of the disco era, and I loved to dance. While living on Elizabeth Ave., I meet a guy by the name of Wayne Peterson. I met him through a mutual friend named Delmar Walker, who I knew from Broome St. in my youth and before the military.

He had gotten drafted by the Army and me by the Marines. Delmar lived down the street from me and he introduced Wayne and me. We began going to parties together and Bruce, another friend from Broome Street, lived a few blocks from us, so the four of us started hanging out together. Wayne and Del were separated from their wives, but Bruce and I weren't. So we formed the Four Musketeers.

On weekends we would party with drugs and music. Wayne and I were the dancers and Bruce and Del, the DJs. Now my Gracie was not a party person; she only liked to go to bingo and drink beer. I hung out with the fellows, but would come home at the end of the party. Doing drugs and drinking a little led me down a path of destruction. I knew that staying out late and even later on weekends, knowing in my heart that it was wrong and that I wasn't treating my wife right. I spent time with people I had no business being with. Then, as time went on at Western, I ask for a raise in pay. I had not gotten a pay increase in pay along with my promotion. When I asked the Residential Supervisor for a raise, he said that he couldn't because of the union rules. I said *all I'm asking for is another quarter or so raise,* and he said that he couldn't. Well this didn't sit too well with me. At this time, I had been employed there for about four years. I had another friend that worked for American Cyanamid, a very large pharmaceutical and chemical company, based in Linden, New Jersey. He said to me one weekend that I should go and apply for a job, that they were hiring. Starting pay, $11.00 dollars an hour. This was $4.50 more an hour then Western was giving me. So I took a day off and went and applied for the job with his recommendations.

I had to take a physical and it was a complete physical, including hearing and all of the other parts of a complete physical. This was when I found out that I had a hearing deficiency in my left ear. I didn't know that it was from Viet Nam. They hired me after I passed the physical. I went back to work the next day and gave a two-week notice to the previous company. This made the supervisor very angry. I reminded him that I had asked for a quarter raise and he's said that he couldn't do it because of the union. So, after a week of some harassment from him, I quit and walked away from pest control. However, it was now in my blood.

I worked at Cyanamid for three months making killer money. I could work all the overtime I wanted working sixteen hours a day in the Malathion Dept. These chemicals were being sent to Karachi, Pakistan for farm use. Now after that big order was complete, we were laid off. I was used to $700 and $800 take home pay, that suddenly disappeared.

However, the supervisor took a liking to me and recommended another company to go to for a job with recommendations. That was Driver Harris Specialty Steel Co. In order to obtain employment from this company, one needed to have very good references. I went for the job application and they told me that they would call. I didn't wait for them to call me; I was persistent and called them every other day asking about employment. I'm sure they were tired of me bugging them this way. But it was my way of showing them that I wanted the job. They hired me for the third shift after training for a week. I didn't like the third shift at all. But I was making eleven dollars an hour again and I put up with the buggy lugging work. All of the equipment was very old. The overhead crane was so old that I had to pull it on the steel beams above the annealing oven that I operated, annealing very costly wire that was used in space ships and any components that needed a wire that could handle very high temperatures, like clothes dryers, spark plugs, etc.

This type of physical work soon put muscles where I didn't have them before. After the shutdown of the plant for two weeks during that first summer, they gave the new employees the opportunity to work through the two-week shut-down at overtime rates; this meant making about $16.50 an hour. Of course, I said *yes* and worked the two weeks doing various odd jobs in the plant, cleaning equipment, oiling machines, and sweeping up debris. Soon after the shutdown was over, I bid on a different job in another department. This was the wire slitting department. Very dangerous. You could get cut real bad operating the old machines; however, they put me with a seasoned operator as a helper. While working in various jobs at Driver Harris, I became a disco party guy, going out every weekend, spending my money on drugs and women instead of saving and preparing for the future. One night, after I had been doing this for a while, I was on the dance floor with a woman and I heard a voice in my head saying, "Walter, what are you doing here? You have a good wife at home and two beautiful daughters." Well when I heard this, it really turned my night upside down. I could not stay in the club, so I went home feeling real bad about my experience. I knew it was God getting my attention. I went home and it was only about 12:30 or 1:00 o'clock in the morning. Too early for Disco Danny to normally be home.

When I got home, Gracie was sitting at the table crying. She asked, "What happened? You didn't have a good time?" This made me feel even worse. And then she uttered these words, "Walter, I'm praying that the Lord would change your heart."

I replied, "Baby don't give up on me, I'm going to change. One day, I will buy you a home and put a fur coat on your back, a diamond ring on your finger and buy a new car for you to drive." My wife just looked at me with disdain and disbelief. She turned and went into the bedroom crying and didn't say a word. I went to bed, but thought intensely about how she looked at me and I prayed that my words would come to pass.

In a few days, I felt the urge to start looking to buy a home and stop paying rent. So, I had been saving bonds on the job and had enough to help with the closing. So we start looking in the Sunday Star Ledger Newspaper for ads. We told God, that if He blessed us with a home, we would start going to church.

This was a deal, so I thought. How many of us should know that we can't make deals with God without Him getting what He wants from us?

I also tried to stop smoking weed and would go for a month or so, but I noticed that, when I'd stop smoking, my drinking would increase and that was a *no* for me. So I went to see my dad, who by now was really bad off. He and my stepmother were separated and getting a divorce. He had his own apartment but, because of his drinking habit, the owners were evicting him. I couldn't let him be on the streets, so I asked Gracie if he could come live with us and she said *yes*. My father would be fine all during the month and stayed sober until the first of the month when he would get his VA check. He would leave sober and come back falling down drunk. This caused a lot of stress on my marriage. My oldest daughter wasn't afraid of him, but Ishia was. One day she found his bottle of vodka and poured it out and filled it with water. When he went to his bottle for a drink, well… it wasn't pretty.

He yelled at her and she started crying. When I got home, we had a heated discussion about his drinking around my daughters. The very next month, I came home from work and he had some guy he'd met drinking somewhere. He'd brought a stranger from a bar into my house. Oh, this made me really angry and I told him if he did that again, he would not be welcomed in my home. So he didn't bring anyone else in.

But a couple of weeks later, Gracie and I decided to go upstate New York to visit my Aunt Cecilia and her husband, Stanley. This meant my daughters were going to Gracie's brother's house for the weekend and dad was staying home. I reminded him, *no visitors at all.* So the weekend was over and we headed home to find a broken living room window and blood on our brand new sofa.

I said to Gracie, "That's it. He's my father, but he has to go." He told us that he couldn't find his key and this was the only way he could get in, when all he had to do was go around back and get in through my daughter's window, which was above a Belcor basement entry. All you had to do was lift up the hinged door and crawl in. I was really sad about my next move; I told my father that we had to break our agreement. I took him to a hotel and dropped him off. I still feel the aftereffects of that day. Our relationship changed from that day, but my father was causing big trouble in my household, between my wife, children, and myself. I had to replace the windows, both storm and regular window, also clean the blood off of the sofa from his cut. Thank God the cut wasn't too bad. From that day, I saw my father only on occasion. He met some lady and moved in with her. I would go by on occasion to see him, he was still my father and I did love him in my heart.

I told myself as a young man that, when I got married and had children, no one would raise them but me. I recalled my childhood upbringing and didn't want that for my children. Now some of the same antics that my father had done when I lived with him, I was doing to my wife and children. I snapped at Gracie over minuscule things, not knowing why I was doing it. When I first came home from 'Nam, I took Gracie to Louisiana to meet my Grammo, and she was carrying Quanika and heavily going toward labor.

My Grammo told her all about how to care for the baby when she would deliver her. She fell in love with Gracie and Gracie with her. One day my Grammo said to me, "Li'l Duke, why you fuss at her so much? She's a good girl, stop fussing at her so much."

I heard her and tried to comply, not knowing that I was suffering from P.T.S.D. My other grandmother, Momma's mother, who we called Mom Ole' fell in love with Gracie as well. Gracie was very likeable. My grandfather loved Gracie as well. Now, on Smith Street, we had some good moments. It was Christmas time 1978, Gracie and I went out to purchase our children's toys. We went bonkers on toys. We bought every toy that they wanted, this was the best Christmas that my girls had ever had. I stayed up all night putting toys together.

The next morning, they were so happy opening their gifts, it did my heart all the good in the world, knowing that, in my childhood, Christmas was a blur. As I think back to my childhood Christmas, receiving a bike was the biggest gift ever. I often reminisce on this gift and still enjoy sharing my elation with my family. Again. it did my heart all the good in the world to buy all those toys, and know that it would make them so happy. Nevertheless, I decided that I would go to my home town for Christmas and leave my family home alone to celebrate Christmas by themselves. How selfish I was. When I think back to those days, I cringe with disdain of my actions. This was Christmas of 1978. After coming back from Louisiana and partying down there with old classmates, I began on a journey of Disco and partying just about every weekend.

During this time, I'd been partying and messing around with people and places that I shouldn't have, I began to feel a pull. During the summer of 1980, while on shutdown from Driver Harris, Gracie and I decided to return to California for a two-week vacation. It had been six years since we'd left the west coast for Jersey and things had changed a whole lot. Prices had gone up exponentially, homes, events, and restaurants. We stayed with Ronald Dean at first and then Pete and on to my uncle, Richard Dale. We enjoyed the time with relatives and returned home feeling good about our trip out west, when all the time I wished that we could have stayed when we lived out there.

After coming back home, we continued working and I continued doing the wrong things. The promise that we made to God for the house, I tried to keep up my end of the bargain. I would go to my stepdad's church, because by this time, he was pastoring his own church and he build it from a small machine shop into a very nice brick church. So, we would go on Sunday, maybe twice a month, not realizing that God was at work on my heart. Every time I would go over to my mother's for a visit, she would talk about Jesus and I would listen, but hurry up and change the subject.

One day, my friend Wayne called my house and told me that he had gotten saved and joined the church. Well, this was big news to me, because at the time, Wayne had a $500.00 a day drug habit. I had started distancing myself from him and had not heard from him in months. I listened to his testimony, congratulated him, and hung up. I said to myself, *if God could save him I know that there is something to this thing called salvation.*

I continued my escapades outside of my home. I would work hard on my job, providing the necessary provisions for my family. I would stay home during the week, just jogging during the evenings and going to Orange Park to hang out with other weed heads. But I would go to the disco on weekends to dance and drink. Well, when 1981 rolled around, we went back to Louisiana to visit my grandparents – my mother's family. We drove my 1978 Ford LTD down there. This car rode like a Lincoln Town Car on the highway. We arrived at my grandfather's. He was an auto body repairman for the Ford dealership in Natchitoches.

He said, "Now, this is a car."

I took him for a ride and he loved it, telling me that he was proud of me and how I had turned out. Having a family and good job, and a nice car. Unaware to me, the prophecy that I had as a child was coming to pass. I had a good wife, two children and a good job, with a nice car. By this time, my Grammo had been with the Lord for eight years. She'd passed while I was stationed in California, 1973, the year Ishia was born and no one informed me of her death. This was very upsetting to me, but I didn't hold any grudges against anyone.

On our way back to Jersey, I stopped in DeRidder to see Aunt Eunice, she was in the hospital with knee surgery and very surprised to see me. We stayed in her house overnight and departed the next morning. I am so happy that the Lord didn't allow me to be bitter towards any of my relatives. He took all malice and hatred out of my heart and this was before I met Him as my personal Savior.

All the time when I was going along, my actions were that of a sinner, I would say to myself, *When I get saved, that I would be truly saved and not a hypocrite.* So, back to Jersey and work. Then 1982 came in and that June, toward the end of the month, my grandmother was diagnosed with colon cancer. Aunt Cecilia and family came down from upstate New York and stopped by my house, picked me up, and we drove down to Louisiana together to be with her in her final days. Getting with my uncles while there, we would smoke and drink, waiting on her demise.

Now they had put me in the room at my cousin Glenda's home. I had a roommate, my sister Dorothy, who was a devout Christian. One night I came in high and she said to me, "Walter, why you do the things that you do? You should give your life to the Lord and be saved."

That was the last thing that I wanted to hear. I said to myself," *They put me in here with her"*. But her words struck a chord with me. When I returned back home from my grandmother's funeral, I began to think about what my sister had said to me that night. I didn't dwell on it too much, but once in a while, I would. In May of 1982, the Lord had blessed us with 104 Lenox Street, our first home. Now here is the last prophecy.

Six days before I turned thirty-one, we moved into that house. I had said when I was a child that, by the time I reach thirty, I would own a house. All of this was given to me by the Lord for a purpose. So now, while I was working at Driver Harris and doing my thing, something started happening. I began to go to church more because of my vow to God. My urge to go out, dancing and drinking, started to dissipate. However, I would smoke and drink at home. While working at Driver Harris, I studied for my State Pest Control License. The more I studied, the more I wanted to get back to the industry. One day while looking in the newspaper's want ads, I saw it.

Pest professionals wanted to make up to $50,000.00 a year, with company car and paid vacations. For all experienced professionals in sales.

Wow, I said, *this is my opportunity to get back into Pest Control.* The company had an office in Fairfield, N.J. and I got all dressed up and went for an interview. I had taken the test earlier and passed. It was a very difficult test, but I passed, only missing a couple of questions. I was licensed in N.J. The gentleman that interviewed me was so impressed with my experience at Western and knowledge of entomology, that he hired me on the spot. I went home to tell Gracie of my new job and that I was leaving Driver Harris. I gave them my notice and started working for this company.

I cannot mention the name in this book, but they are one of the largest in the world, with branches in Europe. After getting a car and going out with other salesman, I noticed the ineptness of the salesman. Also, the chemical supply room was in total disarray.

I said, "Oh boy, what I have done?" I worked for them for a month and had to quit because of the unbelievable things I witnessed. Western was a very professional and organized company and I saw none of that here. I had a mortgage and two children in private school. *What am I going to do now?* I called Driver Harris and they told me that once an employee resigns from the company, they can't rehire them. I was floored and very disappointed. Now, I didn't have a job. I didn't know that God was at work. Every job I applied for – even with my credentials – would not hire me. So to help out with the bills, I would do anything to make a few dollars, working on the garbage truck one day, painting for people from Gracie's job. She worked at Kings Supermarket's headquarters in West Caldwell, N.J. as an assistant grocery buyer. So she was carrying the load of the household. We got behind on our mortgage payments and couldn't make the payments on time and got further and further behind. To relieve the stress on my mind, I would go running for seven to ten miles every day. I didn't realize it, but I found myself praying to God for help, not knowing that it was him blocking all of my efforts of finding employment.

After returning home from running, I would drink a high ball and smoke weed. I had some pest control equipment and tried to start my own business, even that God wouldn't let that prosper. I was desperate, not knowing what to do. The winter came and there was no oil in the tank. The house was freezing, so we all piled up in our bed for warmth with a space heater. My wife would get up and heat water on the stove so that we could wash up and the girls can go to school. These were bad times that I believe that was caused by me, the head of the family. Gracie told me later on that I was driving her to a nervous breakdown with my yelling and snapping at everybody.

I stopped going out and stayed home drinking and smoking weed. We got behind twelve months on the mortgage payments. The mortgage company called every day, but because it was a VA secured loan, they had problems foreclosing on us.

One day, my brother called me and said, "Hey man! I've got some TI stick weed, so why don't you come down and get high with me?"

So I said, "Okay." On my way to his house, I said to myself, *This is the last time that I'm going to get high.* When I arrived at his house with a pint of Yukon Jack, a type of Canadian Whiskey, I told my brother Jesse, "Man, this is the last time that I'm going to get high."

By this time I realized that nothing that I was going to do would get me out of this situation but God. After leaving his house, on the way out the door, he said, "Man, I know you are kidding about not smoking anymore."

I told him I was not kidding. I was so high going home that I was glad that we only lived a few blocks from each other. The next week, all week long while running and praying, I felt something good was about to happen. I thought a job was coming and things would certainly get better. That Friday, while I was out running, the phone rang. Wayne calling for me. When I got back, Gracie said Wayne wants you to call him, immediately, I knew what he wanted. He wouldn't call me but every now and then. This time I knew that he wanted me to go to church with him. I called him back and it was exactly what I thought.

I said, "Yes, I will, what time is service?"

Chapter Eight

THE CHURCH WAS A converted Hebrew Temple. When I walked in, it was the most beautiful place that I had ever seen. But what I didn't realize was that it was the presence of the Lord and His anointing upon the people of God that I was witnessing. The preacher preached a message of forgiveness and healing. When the altar call came and he made the invitation for salvation, I ran up to the altar screaming and crying for God to save me. I didn't care about the people watching or what they thought of me. All I knew was I wanted relief and release from my bondage. I cried for a while and he led me into salvation.

Every time that I think of that night at the altar, when I received Christ into my heart for real, I get emotional and cry. Even after thirty-seven years of walking with God. Now I had tried in my own power to stop doing the things that caused me to sin. I tried on my own to quit smoking and drinking and running around on my wife. But this time, I tried Jesus and He took the taste of drugs that had a hold of me. He took the taste out of my mouth and out of my life. On a Friday night, the pastor of the church asked me to come Sunday to be baptized and I said, *Of course.*

The next day I was tried by the devil. My wife wanted my stepbrother's wife to fix her hair and ask me to take her over there, so I did. We got to the house and his wife said that the two of them were up in the loft shooting pool. This was Jesse and Ronnie Elder Pringle's son. So, I went up and soon as I got up there, I could smell the odor of weed. I didn't pay any attention to it. My brother Jesse rolled up a joint and asks me to light it, or *fire it up*, as the term was in those days.

I replied, "No thanks. I quit and got saved last night."

"What!" Ronnie said, "You, Walter, you got saved?"

Oh, they had a good laugh. Now all of us attended pop's church, but many weren't saved. But, I was saved and being tested. They kept asking and demanding me to fire it up, so I yielded to their demands. When I put the joint in my mouth and lit it, it was the most disgusting thing I had ever tasted in my life.

I gave it back to my brother and said, "That's it; it's not for me anymore." God had taken the taste out of my mouth for good, oh praise God for deliverance from drugs and alcohol. Yes! I called Pastor Pringle and said, "Pop, I got saved last night and I want to go back to that church and get baptized."

He had so much joy for me, but my wife and mother were saying in their hearts, *Well, I've got to see it before believing it.* That Sunday, Quanika and I went to Faith Temple Church and I was baptized and submerged in water. I came up screaming again. After service was over, my friend Wayne asked me to come Wednesday evening for the tarrying service to receive the gift of the Holy Ghost, I said *yes.* I knew in my spirit that I needed Him in order to live this life and, without Him, I would eventually go back to the world.

When my daughter and I got outside, it was the most beautiful day that I had ever seen. It was a spring day in May of 1983. A new beginning for my family and me. When I got home, my wife looked at me and said that I looked different. She came to me and hugged me oh so gently and said, "I'm so happy for this, my husband has been changed." We had dinner and talked awhile about my experience with receiving Christ and baptism.

The next three days, I was on cloud nine with joy, all of the stress was gone. Stress from fear of losing the house, the job that I wanted and much-needed money that would fix a whole lot of things. All of that was gone and I didn't worry about it. Peace came into my life even in the midst of a storm and also gave me the joy that I'd looked for in the wrong places. I saw the most beautiful woman that God had given me in my youth standing before me. I would cry every time that I thought of all the wrong that I had done to her and yet she still forgave me. I told her that for the rest of my life I would try and make up for the wrong things that I had done.

That Wednesday night, I sat at the table in anticipation. I was looking forward to going back to church to receive the gift of promise, the Holy Ghost. Just as Grace put the plates on the table, the phone rang and it was Wayne.

He said, "You didn't eat, did you?"

I said, "Man, my plate was just sat in front of me."

"Oh no," he cried, "don't eat, you want to be empty for the baptism of the Spirit." I jumped up from the table and went out to the church to meet Wayne. We went into a small room, and there were other seekers present. I didn't know what to expect... heaven to open up, angels to appear, Jesus to show up. I just wanted the Holy Ghost. The leaders and my friend said that in order to receive the Spirit, I had to give God the highest praise as loud and fast as I could without letting the devil put doubt in my mind.

So we all started giving God the highest praise, which is hallelujah. Before I knew it after only about a half hour, I was speaking in tongues as the Spirit gave utterance. I was trying to say *hallelujah* but another language came out. I spoke for another half hour straight. We quieted down and I tried to testify as to what happened to me and couldn't talk for the tongues came back stronger. Oh my God, what a miracle this was for this old weed and alcohol head. God not only saved me, but He also baptized me with the power to hold on to my salvation, now I'm sealed unto the day of redemption. Brand new!

I was taught by Pastor Pringle, if there is no change in your actions and habits, then there is no change in you. When I returned to the House of Prayer Church that next Sunday, my mother just kept staring at me to see what she could detect in my action in worship. I could not contain my emotions for joy flooded my soul. When the music went forth, it was the sweetest sound. I began to jump straight up and down, trying to touch the ceiling. My mother, who sang in the choir, was looking at me with tears of joy for what she saw. You see, all of the months that my wife and family attended services, she had never seen me do any real praising of our God. I would go to church sometimes high on weed and just enjoyed the music only, but when the pastor stood up to preach the Word of God, I would try to turn that portion of service off and not let it penetrate my heart. I would leave church sober after the Word and go right out from church and go home have dinner with my wife and children, and then go out and commit sin.

But now, I was brand new and joy filled my soul. I would just cry and give God all of the worship and praise due His Great Name! Now the man I call Pop, and no longer Elder Pringle, my mother's husband, said to me after service that Sunday, "Son."

He called me *son!*

He continued, "Are you going to leave House of Prayer and go to the church that you got saved in? If you do, I would understand."

I said, "Pop, no way am I going anywhere, this is my church and you are my pastor and spiritual leader."

The biggest smile came on his face and he said, "That's good, because that's what I thought."

Now our relationship made a very large shift from that day on. Gracie joined the choir and Quanika was a junior nurse. Ishia sang in the youth choir. I was so happy in the newfound salvation. I didn't have a job, I didn't have any money, I didn't have any more friends except my friend Wayne Peterson, who led me to salvation without harassment. But I had joy, unspeakable joy and was full of glory. I saw my Gracie in a whole new light. My daughters as little princesses. Oh, what joy this was. Now my faith began to give me to start speaking things into existence. The odd jobs that I would do, I would give tithes every Sunday to the church, and sometimes it would be only five dollars.

Gracie said, "That's all you made... why are you giving tithe on that little money?"

And I would tell her, "It belongs to God."

She never again asked me that question about my giving. One Sunday, during the offering time, I prayed a prayer as I watched the deacons and other men in the church give big offerings. I said, "Lord, if you bless me with a good job, I will give like those men. I want to be a blessing to the church." The first job that the Lord gave me was working for King's Supermarkets in Livingston, N.J. as a produce clerk. I didn't like the job, but it gave me the opportunity to bring some money into the house. We were very much behind in our mortgage payments but still happy in our relationship with the Lord.

Every day on my lunch break, I would read my Scofield Bible in my car. I would pray and give thanks for the Word and for the job. I didn't make much money, but we had an income.

But, because I had my pest control license, I would do small jobs in the evening or morning before going to work at the market. I was reminded to not despise small beginnings. We had only one car and it was not in the best shape by now but still running well enough to get us to work. Gracie would drop me off at King's Supermarket and go on to headquarters to work. In the afternoon, I would run home to Lenox Street. This was about 9.5 miles from the store. This was my opportunity to pray and talk to God about my future in Him. I would go into the bathroom at work change into my jogging clothes and my coworkers would ask why I was putting jogging clothes on? *Are you kidding, you are going to run all the way to Newark from here?*

"Yes," I replied.

"It's almost ten miles."

"Don't worry about me; I'm in shape for the run."

The next day the same thing all over again. Soon after, I meet a young man on the job whose father was an electrical engineer and he had all kinds of equipment for testing electrical components. I ask him if he would take my 4-channel Heathkit and check it to see if I had any problems with it. When I'd stopped working on it in California, I had taken it as far as I could without this testing equipment. When he returned the receiver to me, he said that his dad said that I had done a real good job building this kit and I had only two solder bridges on the circuit boards. He fixed it and the amp worked fine.

Wow, all of that soldering paid off. I was so proud of myself. Every day after work I would run home, praying all the way up the mountains of South Orange and part of Short Hills. I would do this run in about an hour and fifteen minutes. I was in really good shape. I wore a size 38 suit jacket and 33 waist. When I gave my life to the Lord, I had only one suit. One day as I passed through So. Orange, N.J. I noticed a consignment store where all the rich Jewish men would bring their expensive suits and ties for charity. I went back to the store later that day and checked out the suits. I found about three suits for five dollars apiece. I took them to a tailor for alterations. These were top quality suits. Thomas Begg, Oli Cassini, and other name-brand suits. When I started wearing them to church, everybody was telling me that I looked very dapper. I went back and purchased more. The lady in the store said that I had purchased all of her good stuff; I laughed and left with two more suits.

As time went on, I kept working at the store as a produce clerk. One day at home, I felt the Spirit say, *Pick up the phone book and look in the yellow pages.*

"Yellow pages," I said to myself, but proceeded to do what the Holy Spirit was prompting me to do. Orkin Termite and Pest Control had just come into New Jersey from Atlanta, GA. I had never seen their advertisement before in the yellow pages. I know that this was God moving on my behalf after about six months from my prayer in that church service. So, I picked up the phone and called. The regional manager answered the phone, and after I told him that I had experience and license for category 7A and 7B. He flipped and asked when I could come in for an interview. I said, *tomorrow morning.* I put a suit and tie on and went for the interview, fasting and praying for victory.

Before the interview was half over, he said to me, "When can you start?"

I said, "I have my own equipment and can start tomorrow."

They gave me a little pickup truck and started me working on the largest route. It was very satisfying to have a good job now. I told Gracie of my good blessing and that evening, we prayed and thanked God for what He had done.

In the state of New Jersey, in order to file bankruptcy, you have to make enough to show that you can pay a certain amount of your debt. I was able now to file and start some kind of repayment of all debts. We found a lawyer and filed, got approved by the courts and began to pay what was asked of us. As time went on, we were challenged in our faith. The mortgage company called one day and said that we had missed a payment and we had to report to the superior court of New Jersey for foreclosure proceedings. The first time that we went down to the courts, the judge was not there and they postponed the hearing. We went the second time and it happened again. The third time, we fasted and prayed each time, but this time we called on the Lord with fervent prayer and asked God as before to vindicate us. We could not find the money order receipt for the month that was at question. We had all others in our possession but that one. When the circuit court judge came into the courtroom, he had a serious expression and we held hands and started to pray. The lawyers for the mortgage company were looking at us real hard as if to strike fear into our hearts. But we were standing firm on God's Word that He would never leave us nor forsake us. We knew that we were not guilty of missing any payments but could not prove it without the receipts. The lady in front of us was next and the judge foreclosed on her house right away. She left out of the courtroom, crying. We felt so bad for her.

Then we were next, but before the bailiff could call our names, our lawyer and the mortgage company's lawyer came in the courtroom and beckoned for us to come out into the hallway. The mortgage company lawyer said, "Mr. and Mrs. Dukes, we found the missing payment, so just keep up the payments on time and you will be okay."

My wife and I looked at each other and began to cry and praise God for the victory. We were told that we didn't have to go back into the courtroom. I give God all the glory for the victory through Christ Jesus. The devil thought he had us, but

God vindicated us and gave us the victory. When we got in the car, the Holy Spirit reminded me that it was only a test of our faith in our God. We knew from that moment on that all of the money order receipts had to be filed. We didn't have a checking account as of yet, so receipts were quite important.

As time went on, the job at Orkin was working out well and, on Saturdays, I would do side jobs for different companies. My mother and pop were very encouraging to us. Our car finally gave out and all we had was the little work truck to go to church in. Gracie would catch rides with a co-worker. After about nine months of working the routes and cleaning them up from a major lack of service, the regional manager called me into a meeting and offered me a management position as service manager. I accepted the position even though it was a salaried position with a company car.

As time moved toward Christmas of 1984 and we were keeping track of our responsibilities with bills and the household. A week before Christmas, I got a call from Louisiana. It was my aunt, my father's brother's wife. She said that my father, who by now had moved down to Jackson, Louisiana, to live in a veteran's home, had been shot by robbers.

He was dead.

This was terrible news, especially at Christmas time. I went to the branch manager and ask permission to drive my company car down to Louisiana. He said, *Of course.* Before I made plans to get on the road, Pop asked me if I had money to go. Gracie and I had saved up some money to purchase a new dinette set, but every time we started to go buy it, something would come up and we'd have to postpone the trip to the furniture store. This was God blocking our plans so that, at this moment in time, that we would need the money for this emergency.

Pop said, "Son, I want you to take my credit card for emergency use."

I told him that we were okay to travel. When I think of the man of God that he truly was, it encourages me that he passed through my life. Another time, before I had given my life completely over to God, I developed a very serious rash or blisters on the soles of my feet, which I believe came from my time in the jungles of Viet Nam. I went to the VA hospital and they didn't know how to treat it or what it was, so they gave me soaks and ointments, which didn't work. So I went to a dermatologist and he couldn't identify it either. The blisters or lesions were getting worse. A thought came to me – *Go to Pop Pringle and get him to pray and anoint your feet.* I know now that the words were the Holy Spirit speaking to me into my mind.

So I went over, expecting him to say some great prayer and anoint my feet with blessed oil. He was sitting in his easy chair and he allowed me to tell him the problem. Like Elijah did Naaman, he had me bend over in front of him. He placed his hand on my forehead and prayed silently, not allowing me to hear what he said to God. It took all of about two minutes. I left his presence and the next day, the blisters were gone, never to come back in force to this day, praise God. I found out that the blisters were a form of jungle rot from the 'Nam. Thank God for that man of God.

We got on the road early in the morning and started towards Louisiana when it dawned on me that God had given me the promotion because, first He knew that the old Ford was on its last legs and that I would need a car for this purpose. Some would say *No, it was just a coincidence.* But God was at work. My children were very sad going down because they knew their Christmas was on hold. We took my little brother Cecil with us and arrived in Natchitoches.

Even though my father and stepmother were divorced, she still carried him on her insurance policy and that was a big relief. He had gotten a large settlement check from the VA and was on his way up to Jersey to see us. He stopped in a bar to drink and flashed some money and a man and woman followed him out and robbed him, he hit one of them over the head with his stick and they shot him with a .22 caliber pistol. The wound closed up and he went to a hotel and died there. We had his funeral and came back home.

It was a bad time in our lives. But God brought us through! It hurt me to see my father die this way at only fifty-four years old. But he'd prophesied his own death. When my family would request of him to please stop drinking, he would reply, "Liquor can't kill me, the only thing that can kill me is a bullet."

And that's how he died – alone and in pain. What a sad commentary. I learned later on from the study of God's Word in Proverbs 18:21, "Death and life are in the power of the tongue, and they that love it shall eat the fruit thereof." King James Version.

So, from that point on, I became aware of what came out of my mouth. Working for Orkin gave me the opportunity to meet some nice people. The branch manager was from Virginia and he exclaimed to me that his parents raised him to hate Black people and that he could not understand where this hatred came from. After he had grown up and was on his own, he learned that there were bad people in all races of people and that he learned to judge people by their character. This gave me an insight into his thinking of me. I was second in command at the branch. I was carrying the branch on my license and had nine commercial technicians, nine combo techs, residential and sales, also nine commercial salesmen. Because of my knowledge of pest control techniques, our branch grew in sales and service.

I won the regional sales and service award for the quarter. This prize was a rental car for a three-day weekend.

I told Pop about this event and he again blessed me. He gave me a credit card to rent the car. I rented a brand new Town Car from Hertz and went to Virginia to visit my cousin Elliott Dukes III. What a ride this car had. On the way down, I kept repeating to Gracie, *One day I'm going to have a Lincoln.* As time went on, I became restless and would go out in the field whenever I could get away from the office. I learned something about myself. I didn't like being behind a desk. One day, the regional manager told me that the numbers from my branch weren't coming up to par and that they wanted me to step down as branch service manager and take a commercial sales position, this didn't make me too happy. After all, I was working nights training techs and cleaning up problem accounts.

I asked for a raise being that the branch was under my auspices or authority. Of course, they said *no.* I went to discuss this matter with the man of God. By now, I had been with Orkin for two years and I had a small number of customers of my own. Pop said to me, "Walter, you are one of the best pest control professionals that I've ever known, why don't you open your own business?"

Now this was the spring of 1986 and one of the residential salesmen, named Peter Derogates, had left Orkin to work for a large mortgage company and I had told him about my bankruptcy. The reason I mention this is because I've got to give God some more praise for His grace and mercies. They told us that when we filed for this bankruptcy that we couldn't get any type of credit for ten years. But God put this young man in my presence for the purpose of getting us refinanced with our loan on the house. He took all of the information and went to work and got us refinanced through the company that he worked for.

At the time, I was caught up on my home and children's school responsibilities. I told Pop, "Look, I have a mortgage, children in private school, and I would very much like to be self-employed."

He said to me, "Step out on your faith in the God that you serve. You don't have to work for no one but yourself. If I can do it all these years, so can you." I left and began to pray for direction. The Holy Spirit allowed me to meet people who wanted service, but didn't want the high prices of a large company, so I would tell them that I'm going to start my own business, by now I had a total of eleven years in service, sales, and now management.

Pop said to me, "Son, when I get back from the April call meeting, I will help you get started."

He and Momma went to Memphis driving his brand new conversion van. So I started setting up my company, getting new people that God sent my way. I can remember saying, while working for Western Termite and Pest Control, going into the high-end suburbs of New Jersey, where the elite of the state lived, that one day I would like to have my own company and service these same customers. I didn't know that I was speaking into my own life again. Pop and Momma got back home from a five-day trip to Memphis. When they would go away, Pop would put Gracie and me in charge of the church even though there were other deacons there in ministry. My wife would handle the finances and I would receive the tithe with a seasoned deacon. After I started receiving the offerings and giving bountifully in church, the people would receive what I would say over their giving. Both tithe and offerings increased exponentially and the ministry increased in the church coffers. I called Momma and she said that Pop didn't feel well and that he has heartburn from eating peanuts on the road; this was Friday evening. Saturday morning, she called me and said he wasn't doing well at all and if he didn't improve, she would take him to the emergency room. So I waited and she called me back and said that they kept him and that he'd had a heart attack on the highway. This made me very upset in my spirit and I went to the hospital with Gracie, on the way there, I recalled the times that he, along with Momma, would pick us up for the ride to Plainfield, a twenty-mile journey from Newark. On the way one morning, he said the exact words Grammo said to me about fussing at Gracie.

Chapter Nine

Pop said, "Son you've got a good wife, stop fussing at her so much." This rang a very large alarm in my spirit, because the same words had come from my Grammo earlier, in 1971. Then I realized that I had a major problem with temperance, so I began to pray and ask God for help with self-control, one of the fruits of the Spirit that I needed so desperately.

In the three years that I've been saved now, that problem hung on. This was one of the symptoms of P.T.S.D. that I had but didn't know it as of yet. For three years, Pop and I grew closer, even more than with his four sons. We would go and eat together on Saturdays while my mother and Gracie were at choir rehearsals and shopping. They became like mother and daughter. Pop would call me on Saturday after getting in from servicing my few customers. He would ask what I was doing. He'd come and pick me up and we would go to Ground Round Restaurant on Route 22.

So on the way to the hospital, all of these thoughts flooded my mind. This man of God is my pop as well as my pastor. *I need him in my life*, I told God. Arriving at the hospital, He said to me, "Go to church tomorrow and take care of the church."

At his bedside, I said, "Pop, I want to be here with you."

He said, "Go to the church."

So that Sunday morning, I went as he had said. The next week I left Orkin to start Wings Pest Control. This was my nickname in Viet Nam, *Baby Wings*. So it was an appropriate name for a pest control business. I went to the hospital to let him know that I'd quit my job at Orkin and now I was on my own, trusting in God for directions.

He said, "Wonderful, I'm going to help you buy a truck."

Well, Friday came and I was going to start full-time that day, April 18th 1986. I went to my first customer's home using the car that I had saved up for, the one for Gracie to get back and forth to work in. In those days, we didn't have cell phones, nor did I have a pager. I left my first customer in Oakland N.J. and headed to Short Hills to service a large, upscale home for pavement ants that the previous company couldn't get rid of.

From there, I headed south to Marlboro, N.J., an hour from where I was in Short Hills. I gave Gracie my route schedule. By the time I reached the home, the wife came to the door and said for me to call home – it was urgent. I called Gracie and said, "What's wrong?"

She said, "Come home right away, Pop died in the hospital and Momma is going out of her mind."

I dropped everything and tried to compose myself in front of the customer and she said to me, "Go, see about your family." It was about a forty-five-minute ride to Newark and all I could think of was, *What am I going to do now, my mentor, my pop, my pastor has just died and he's only fifty six.* I arrived at my mother's and she met me at the door with all of my siblings waiting for me to get there. She fell in my arms and cried so loudly and wept profusely. I knew that all the responsibility would fall on me. My mother relied on me to handle all of the business of the funeral arrangements and banking. Before going to Memphis, Pop had gone to Ray Catino Mercedes Benz dealership to get a new car. I took my mother there to retrieve the two-thousand dollar down payment to order the car. The next day after all the arrangements were complete, my family and I gathered together to mourn our loss.

At this time in my life, the whole family was looking to me for strength and leadership. So I would pray and ask the Lord for direction and strength. The day of the home going service came. It was one of the largest services that I had ever witnessed; the church that it was held at was filled to capacity, around 1200 people. The procession to the graveyard had a line of cars three miles long going through the city. My pop was well known throughout the brotherhood, including our headquarters, Memphis, Tennessee. After the funeral and well wishes were over, I had to contend with the church and our jurisdictional Bishop, Bishop Chandler David Owens.

He instructed me to hold the church together until a new pastor could be appointed. Here I was a new deacon, not even ordained yet and I've got the responsibility of the church that had, at that time, about 200 active members. The Sunday after the funeral, I went to the church after getting directions from the Bishop. I went into Pop's quarters and fell down on my knees and wept profusely, crying out to God asking Him what I going to do now that my pop and pastor was gone, my mentor and friend.

We had become so close by this time and he was grooming me for ministry even though I didn't know it. He had told my mother that he saw me becoming a minister and told her not to tell me. I wondered why he would get to the church before anyone else and send me for coffee. He would take me around the church's exterior and tell me his extension plans of acquiring the next-door property. All of this was gone now. What was I to do? I got all of my weeping and sorrow out in those quarters that morning; the Holy Spirit lifted me and gave me purpose that same day.

Different elders would come to minister to us the Word of God, and there were two elders that were attending our church, but not members yet, they also would preach as the bishop would appoint them. One day, the bishop called me and said, "Deacon Dukes, if you don't approve of the elders that call you for an appointment, and they want to be the minister in the church, it's up to you." This was a grave assignment for a young UN-ordained Deacon.

There were men and women of God coming out of the woodworks wanting that small, beautiful church. The mortgage was just about paid in full and had a large parking lot and amenities. So I would screen the people calling and pray for directions from the Lord. What a responsibility. After about eight months of this large headache for me and others in the church, two members called the bishop and told him that my wife and I were misappropriating funds. All we were doing was saving every dime that came in and paying all of the ministry bills. The bishop sent over a team of elders to look at the books and see what was going on. They came and we opened up all of the books and ledgers of the church. They were so impressed with our record-keeping and bookkeeping skills. They made a report back to the bishop and we were cleared of these charges. I called the bishop and asked him to please send us a pastor. There was a certain elder that the most of the church liked; he had been coming for a while at different times. Elder William T. Cahoon already had a small ministry in Jersey City, but we liked his style of preaching. Bishop Owens, with my family's and my recommendations, appointed him pastor of House of Prayer Church. Some of the old members left the church, but others came and joined, the church was going forward with revivals and consecrations.

My business was also growing and I began to look for a truck. I had saved up my income taxes and some cash from my route. One day after I finished work, the Holy Spirit prompted me to go home and get the money that I had saved up. I followed the Spirit's leading and asked Him where I should go. The Spirit said, "Just start driving." I wound through the streets of Newark, turning where He led me and ended up on Route 22 Hillside, N.J. This was the car dealer's highway. As soon as I crested the hill, I saw a Datsun B 2200 pickup truck right by the highway. If it was any closer to the road, it would have been sitting in the emergency lane at the edge of the road. I pulled over and began to inspect the truck. No one came out of the dealership at first, so I looked at the price of the truck that was plastered on the front windshield, $3,000. I had that amount in my possession. Finally, a young salesman came out and asked if I was interested in that truck. He opened up the truck and inside was air-conditioning, a cassette tape player, and a sunroof that the previous owner had installed.

I said, "Can I take it to my mechanic for evaluation?"

So we drove all the way across town and the mechanic said to buy it. I bargained with the manager after telling him that I just started my business and needed a break on the price so that I can purchase insurance. I paid $2,400 dollars for the truck and drove it off the lot. This, again, was God showing me favor. The truck looked brand new, black with white markings. Just before I received my first carpenter ant job, the Lord blessed me to purchase a new bed top with ladder racks on top. This was very much needed to carry ladders for the jobs. The next day, my first big ant job came in.

Oh, what a happy young Christian I was, seeing all of the miracles that God was doing in my life, and how Pop encouraged me to work for myself. It had come to pass. Orkin was calling me just about every week asking me to return, and telling me what they would give me on my return. By this time, my Lord was opening doors for me. I was getting jobs in suburbia – the million-dollar homes. One rich customer would tell their friends about Wings Pest Control. By the summer of 1988, the business was growing and I couldn't keep up with all of the functions of the home office and field work, so I ask Gracie to leave her job to help me. She gladly consented. Her job was very stressful, dealing with all of the vendors at King's.

One day they had to call for the EMTs to take her to the emergency room; her blood pressure was at stroke level. This was the beginning of her major health challenges. So much work was coming in that I had to hire a helper. My wife's nephew, Dion Way, was available for hire. We'd work from 7:30 until dark all summer long. Gracie and I had never had a real honeymoon and I was thinking of taking her somewhere.

I used to see the commercials of the Caribbean's turquoise waters. One day, the phone rang in the evening and it was a travel scam, telling us that we had won a five-day vacation in the Bahamas and all we had to do was send them $400 dollars for airfare and hotel, well we knew that this was a scam, but Gracie had her hopes up and thought that we were going on a vacation. When we found out the scam was real, we both were so disappointed. I thought to myself, I've got some money saved up; I would love to take her somewhere. She looked in the newspaper and saw the Di Vi –Di Vi travel agency advertising a five-day vacation in Puerto Rico for just under $300 each. It even included hotel and airfare. Wow, what a deal. We made our plans for this trip to the Caribbean. We made provisions for our daughters with Momma and departed on our first real vacation after eighteen years of marriage.

We arrived in San Juan and saw the beautiful water and beaches. The hotel was not all that great, but we didn't care about that, just to be there in paradise was enough for us. This was the first installment of my promise to Gracie that night of my encounter with the Spirit of God on the dance floor. We enjoyed our vacation and brought back souvenirs for everybody in the family, especially Momma and my girls.

Momma and Gracie's relationship grew even closer and as time went on we prospered in our home grown business so much that we had to move out of the house and into an office building in Union, N.J. We hired Momma to file and answer the phone. Gracie even taught her how to type invoices. She was so happy to be doing something out of her home and getting paid for it. The business grew and we landed some large commercial accounts, like the New Jersey Institute of Technology and the City of Irvington Rodent Control contracts, schools, day cares, and restaurants, but my specialty was carpenter ants in the suburbs. This was where the real money was made.

We didn't have to advertise. Word of mouth was how we grew our business. By the late 80s, I felt the call to ministry by God's pulling. While jogging, I found myself preaching to myself. I tried to denounce what God was doing, but the more I resisted, the stronger the call came. I went to the pastor and acknowledged my calling. He gave me a date for what was called my trial sermon. I called my wife's family and my family who didn't attend the church. From this point on, after the sermon was preached, I was called Minister Dukes by the pastor and congregation. I knew that I needed Bible training, so I attended Screven's Bible Institute in Newark, and after that, Moody's Bible Institute of Chicago, Ill.

So after the calling, the two people that I mentioned earlier, the ones who called the bishop concerning the handling of the church funds, they approached me and ask for my forgiveness for their lack of trust. They said that I'd proven my good standards by my actions. I didn't know who it was that had made that call and didn't try to find out, but realized that jealousy played a great part in their decision to call. I quickly moved on from any feelings of dislike or hard feelings.

The Lord was prospering my business and I paid tithes on my gross income of the business. After moving into Union, N.J. The business continued growing and I hired a second technician. In the early nineties, Gracie and I began to go on cruises during the slow season, which began in late October early November. We would cruise the Caribbean Sea, hitting all the Islands, Aruba, Martinique, Granada, Venezuela, Columbia, and other places like the Panama Canal. Remember the promise that I made my wife? The Lord gave me the opportunity to fulfill my promise. On our 25th anniversary, I took her to Los Vegas for a five-day vacation. It was our first experience there. We went out to the Grand Canyon and Hoover Dam. We ate in the best of hotels and returned home. On that trip, I presented her with a diamond anniversary ring. She cried when I reminded her of my promise. My intention of recalling these events to make it known that words have energy and will produce what you speak by faith in God, that's what you are asking for is within His will for your life. You just have to know His Word and that His Word is His will. Keep speaking by faith what you believe is within His will and it shall come to pass.

In June of 1992, I was ordained an elder in the Church Of God In Christ, with all rights and privileges in the church. Bishop Chandler David Owens, a General Board Member of the Church of God in Christ officially ordained me. Wells

Cathedral was the largest C.O.G.I.C. church in the state of N.J. and he was the pastor. It was a great honor to be ordained by this great leader in the church. He was one of the most anointed preachers of his era. The members of House of Prayer church received me as one of the men of God under the leadership of Pastor Cahoon.

By 1994 I felt the calling that was in me to pastor. I felt the calling in my spirit. Through prayer and consecration, I left the church. When Pop died, I didn't have a mentor for advice, but God put someone in my life – Elder H. L. Taylor. He took a liking to me. We were now under a new district lead by Superintendent Cahoon, who was promoted by Bishop Owens. Pastor Taylor's church was a growing and thriving ministry. His Sunday school classes had more students than a lot of churches had members. He was so down to earth and easy to talk to that people were drawn to his love and compassion.

He hired my pest control company to service Born Again Church and daycare. While my technician would service both buildings, he and Elder Charles Harris would talk with me about everything under the sun. We would enjoy the conversations, and so I really admired him. After I got ordained, he had me to come and speak on a Sunday morning for his pastoral anniversary. This was a big deal for me; this was one of the most blessed opportunities that I had as a young elder in the church. I took my family with me and we enjoyed the fellowship. The Lord blessed in the preaching. I was getting my preaching legs, as it was known. We became close; he was like a father to me. I would share my problems and situations with Pastor Taylor and he would give me sound counsel and wise advice. I know that God put this man of God in my life for such a time as that. When I departed House of Prayer to start my own church, I received wise counsel from my mentor. Bishop

Owens had been called by the mother church to Atlanta to take over a jurisdiction where the bishop had died. So we needed a new Jurisdictional bishop. Bishop Cahoon was chosen or voted in as the New Garden State Jurisdictional bishop. Some of the pastors from the old jurisdiction didn't want to be a part of the newly formed jurisdiction. So a new fellowship was formed by those pastors. I was at the beginning of my ministry and knew that I needed a covering.

One day on my route, I saw Elder Prescott on the parkway; he was one of the pastors who came to the church to review the financial statements of the time that pastor Pringle had died. I spoke to him and said that I would like to be a part of the fellowship. He invited me to bring my family and minister to his church that next Sunday. When I departed House of Prayer, I didn't invite anyone from that ministry to follow me out. I knew from the church's protocol that this was not an ethical thing to do. I took my family, which numbered around seventeen to twenty souls. They followed me of their own will and not coercion. We went to his church and ministered there and were well received, very well. Pastor Norman L. Prescott was a highly respected man of God in New Jersey and throughout the brotherhood.

When the April call meeting was scheduled in April 1995, it was my first time going to Memphis. All other times when this time of year would come during my pops and Bishop Cahoon's visits to Memphis either in November Holy Convocation or April call meeting, I had to stay and hold down the church and ministry. This was a whole new experience for me. Pastor Prescott, Pastor Taylor, Pastor Lee, Pastor Harris, and I boarded the plane to Memphis. At this time, our Chief Apostle Bishop Henry Ford had passed and the church was holding his viewing at Mason Temple.

All these events were happening at one time. We were there for our confirmation of being a jurisdiction in the general assembly. We were present during the vote to allow the fellowship to become a jurisdiction in New Jersey. The Third Jurisdiction of New Jersey was formed, and Elder Norman Prescott was chosen as our jurisdictional bishop. We had great fellowship in Memphis, celebrating this milestone in all of our lives. The five of us came home to our local churches rejoicing over this news. The Lord had given me the name of our new ministry after much prayer and seeking God for this name. Genesis Temple C.O.G.I.C. was born in my mother's living room with Bible study and then, as we grew with new people, we moved to my brother Jesse's living room and then to my basement. With continued growth, we found the VFW hall in Kenilworth N.J. The manager said that we could rent every Sunday for two hours.

Soon we were told that other people wanted to rent the space for events such as train shows and other exhibitions, which would block us from having our services there. One day riding up the parkway from a funeral, Gracie and I saw the Kenilworth Inn sign. I said, "Why don't you call and see if they had a room that we could rent to have worship services?"

When she called the manager, he said to her, "I've been waiting on your call, what took you so long?" This made us rejoice to the highest. Here was God showing us again that He was with us. They charged us $900.00 a month for four Sundays and a Thursday night joy night service. We gained new members and enjoyed being a part of the third heard, so I named the Third Jurisdiction of N.J. The spring workers' meeting were unreal in praise and worship of our new beginning as a Jurisdiction and Genesis as a new church in the vineyard of the Lord. We stayed in the hotel for three years and prospered in our savings and membership growth, the people of God were faithful in tithing and offerings. We saved every dime.

I showed the people of God by example that the pastor had to lead out in our giving. I gave tithe on my gross business income and a liberal offering every Sunday and Thursday night offering. God blessed my business and prospered the people of God in their homes and on their jobs as well. After three years in the hotel, it was time for us to have our own space to worship in. We looked high and low for buildings to rent or buy. My wife and mother would go on their lunch breaks from Wings to look for buildings.

One day, driving down the parkway, the Lord spoke to me and said, *Stop looking for a building, I will show you where you are to go.* I called my mother and wife and told them to stop looking, and what the Lord had spoken to me. After a few weeks, the hotel started hinting that they were ready for us to go, even though we were never late with our rent payments. New management had taken over the hotel after they came out of bankruptcy, so they wanted us out.

One Sunday, Gracie was looking in the Sunday Star Ledger Newspaper and saw a commercial building ad, saying that two places were for rent, and could be used as a church. Wow! What a leap in my heart. The Lord had said, *Stand down on looking for a place; He will show us where we are to be.* The first place was on Clinton Ave. Newark, and the other place was downtown Washington Street in the belly of the beast. We went to look at both places the same day. The place on Clinton Ave. didn't appeal to our needs so we ventured downtown to Washington Street. The 3000 square foot place was above an Electronics Store, and they had used the space as an electronics repair school. We had to go through the store to enter the upstairs space. I had encouraged my brother Jesse and his wife Bessie to come along with us.

When we got upstairs, I turned to see their expressions on their faces. Well, Bessie had the look of, *are you kidding me?* Jesse was just standing, looking around with no real expression on his face and Gracie just stood with her eyes closed. I heard the Lord say, "*This is it.*" The space had old broken televisions, VCRs and other electronic equipment scattered throughout the rooms. The ceiling was about twelve feet high with wires running over every inch of the ceiling. But I heard God say, *this is it.* Now the landlord said that they would clean the space out, but it was left up to us to build it into a church. 3000 square feet was a lot of space to work with.

I stood quiet and waited on the Lord to show me how to divide the space up into a worship center for the people of God. He showed me, as I waited, where to put the pulpit and which direction to have the pew chairs. In the Genesis Temple church, we had a few brothers with building skills. My brother Jesse, Deacon David Corley and Brother Rob had the skills to do the work that needed to be done. We had to drop the ceiling, tear down walls and erect walls to make the sanctuary fellowship hall and offices. We had one bathroom and so we made it unisex. We built a kitchen as well. All in this 3000 square feet of space. We rented the space in December and I told the members that by the first Sunday in February, we would have our first Sunday worship in our new place. The men and I, with a few helpers, would get off work every day then go downtown to work in the church until sometimes twelve a.m. or one in the morning. Dion and my son-in-law Teriq would do the helping and food run every night. We got tired of Burger King and fried chicken. I would buy all of the food for the men who worked so hard every night and on Saturdays. I was the painter and material supplier. A total of $16,000 was spent on the renovation of that space.

On the first Sunday of February, we had our first service. We had worked until 3:00 a.m. that Saturday night and went home for a few moments rest and returned for morning worship. No preaching was done that Sunday due to the praise of our God for what He had done for us. Our own place of worship! Here we started off right, adding five new members that Sunday, and growth happened so fast. Here was another example of what God was doing in my life and now my ministry. We had the space for around 125 or 130 worshipers in this space and, on most Sundays, we were full, with new people giving their lives to the Lord and getting saved, healed and delivered from sin.

What a time to be in ministry, I started pastoring at forty-three and the challenges of that task was great. I experienced some very hard sleepless nights on my face, crying out to God for directions for the people of God. With 100 or so faithful members every Sunday, I learned early on that each one had a personality to contend with. Much fasting and praying and seeking God lead me down the path of righteousness. Showing by example to the people how we had to obey God's Word and love each other. Care for one another. We were soon known as the No Nonsense church, and the church of love and compassion. As the Lord increased our borders, He also promoted me in the jurisdiction as well. I became the Sunday School Superintendent for five years. I was the leader until we merged all of the ministries together under the AIM banner – Auxiliaries in Ministries. We were on Washington Street downtown Newark, with a large homeless population; we began to experience our cars being broken into and other petty crimes. We approached the city about parking in the city lot across the street from the building with permits only; this helped with the break-ins. Also, we hired an off-duty police officer for security. This helped tremendously.

Chapter Ten

1998 WAS THE BEGINNING of Gracie's more serious heart issues. October of that year, she spent a week in the hospital. She was my right arm in ministry. The Lord anointed her to have all kinds of ideas for the youth of the church and women's ministries. She was anointed by God to put programs and ministry goals into action. This woman of God was a prayer warrior. When I would preach and minister to the people. I would look at her and her eyes were closed in deep prayer for me and whomever I was ministering to.

One day she said, "Take me to the doctor." For her to say that, I knew she was having some problems. Her heart began to fail. They took pictures of her heart, front and rear through a catheter and we found that she had a serious problem. She spent a week in the hospital and I decided that for her birthday in November I would take her on her favorite vacation, cruising. I booked a twelve-day cruise to the Panama Canal and through it to Mexico. This did both of us all the good in the world to get away from the stresses of ministry and running the company.

By this time, we had people both in the church and the company to take care of things while we were on vacation. The reason that I'm recalling this now, because I want to remind people of my promise to my wife the night that the Lord spoke to me on the disco floor dancing with another woman. The Lord heard what I said to her that night some twenty years earlier. God made the way for me to fulfill my promises to her because I really meant what I told her about the rings, fur coats, and new cars. He allowed me through our business to fulfill these promises and not on the backs of our members. In the beginning, I didn't allow the saints to even give me an offering, every penny went into the bank for ministry.

We started a building fund drive for our own building in 2001. We would save the Thursday Joy night offering, which sometimes would add up to around $500.00 dollars. It didn't take long for us to build that account up. In 2000, the Lord sent a couple, by the name of Walter and Joan Covertinto our ministry that saw the need to have a celebration for the pastor. Of course, I said no, but they got with other people and ministries with in the church and put it together anyway. At that time, I had been pastoring for six years and at the celebration, all of the jurisdictional leaders were present – friends and well-wishers alike. It was a tremendous affair. The church made me feel so much love coming from all of the members that attended. By the way, my high school friend, Paul Ashford and his wife Roslyn attended as well.

The ministry grew and the people were blessed. The average ages of members were about thirty to forty-five years old with a few seniors and a lot of children. The saying goes, if you have a lot of children in the church, you have a growing and alive church, if not, it's a dying church. I found this to be true in so many ways. The youth department would have so many events for the youth of the church that they want to be a part of the church. They would have youth shut-ins and picnics. Youth groups took outings to different places. And every year after school in the month of August, I would take the church on a weekend trip to Busch Gardens in Virginia or some other area. It was mainly for the children who never had the opportunity to experience summer fun away from home. We did this every year during the month of August. My daughters would help out with the task of youth ministry. Quanika and Ishia were a tremendous asset to the ministry. Ishia did her part in the choir and youth events and Quanika was a part of the choir and nurses unit, while helping with the very large youth population of the Genesis Temple Church. We ordained Deacons and had a very strong missionary dept. The Sunday school was led by my mother. She did an excellent job as the superintendent. Every aspect of the church was viable. With my brother's faithfulness to the building of the sanctuary and ministry, and his acknowledgement of his calling to the ministry. I licensed him to preach and, later on, the bishop ordained him an elder in the C.O.G.I.C. faith. He was a tremendous help in ministry. I would leave him in charge of the church when going to Memphis and on vacations.

We had an extraordinary music ministry under his leadership. They ministered to people through their singing and praise. Elder Jesse Pringle played the organ and arranged the music being led by the Spirit. Souls were saved and filled with the Holy Ghost during those formidable years. His son Jesse, Jr. would play the drums under the anointing along with his dad, he also would lead songs and we would have afternoon services where the music ministry would have concerts. What a time in the Lord we would have. Going to minister at other churches in our jurisdictions and out of our jurisdiction, I would be so proud of the Genesis Temple music ministry. Young people from all over the city were coming and joining the ministry.

Now, running a business and pastoring full time was a huge challenge for me. Tuesday night Bible study, Wednesday morning 6:00 a.m. prayer, Thursday night Joy night, and Sunday afternoon services, either at Genesis or other ministries were a tremendous burden on me. I look back at those days, and know that it was God that kept me to keep on keeping me.

By 2003, my wife's health began to deteriorate even more. As she sang in the choir, I noticed that she would get winded after one song. Others in the church would make different comments to me about what they observed during her singing. I soon ask her to step down from the choir. This didn't sit too well with her. She loved to sing, but eventually, she acknowledged her lack of oxygen. By March of 2003, after a few time being taken to the ER, I realized that after all of the medicines and pumps that her primary doctor was prescribing to her they weren't doing her any good. I decided to try a new doctor.

One day on my route, I mentioned to one of my customers, who I felt a friendly connection with, that my wife was suffering with heart problems. He said to me that he had one of the best heart cardiologists in the state, and that at his recommendation, he would take her on as a patient. I rushed to the phone and called my wife with the news. She called Dr. Watsi. He was the head of the cardiology department of Beth Israel Medical center. He told her to come in the next morning. He examined her and told her that she couldn't go home. He admitted her into the hospital that same day. The heart surgeon met with us and said that she needed surgery right away. Her aortic valve and mitral valve were in need of replacement. The aortic was so calcified that a major heart attack was imminent. They scheduled her for surgery the next day. The surgery was a success and she recovered with six weeks in the ICU. My bishop came to the hospital with us and stayed until the surgery was complete. I will now and always remember Bishop Norman L. Prescott for his love and compassion towards my wife and my family during those trying days. She recovered and came home from the hospital with sisters from the church and jurisdiction helping with home health aide work. Mother Roberta Taylor, Pastor Taylor's wife would come to the hospital from Piscataway, N.J., every day to feed her ice chips in the hospital and would visit her often at home during her recovery time. They became so close. Mother Taylor taught my wife the ins and outs of being a pastor's wife, and how to interact with the members of the church. She showed by example how to be a first lady. Pastor and Mother Taylor took us under their wings.

They cared for the both of us and showed it in so many ways, we began to travel to Memphis together every year and Pastor Taylor and I would travel to the leadership conferences, April Call meetings together every year, and when I needed advice about ministry, I would call on him for his long experience and godly council. I started calling him Pop because of the love that he showed my family and me. He called me his son. Now that we were so close, I would visit his home and he ours. My wife was an excellent cook and this went a long way with Pop and Mom Taylor. We would go out to different restaurants together as well. Soon we became very close to each other and our families as well.

By the first of July, my wife was walking around at Disneyland in California. My relatives out there could not believe that she had recovered so quickly. We took our family out there on vacation for my grandson's sixth birthday celebration. Dominique Dukes Davis my only grandchild at the time, his mother Ishia and her husband Teriq was expecting their second child at the time. We enjoyed the family time together. We visited my family and went to the main attractions, Sea World, Disneyland, and the San Diego Zoo. When we returned home, all was well at the church and with the business as well. But when she reported back to the cardiologist, he informed her that the blood thinner she was on needed to be increased because of her mechanical valves and that she had to be checked every two weeks. This started taking a toll on her, going back and forth to the clinic all the time. Doctor's appointments, blood labs, and the heart clinic were the way of life for my wife. Her heart, in spite of the major operation that she'd had, was still getting weaker by the month.

Gracie was feeling good in her body after the recovery from the major operation that she had. I want to point out something here. If the Lord had not directed me to seek out another doctor, my wife would have had a major heart attack. The surgery lead doctor told me personally that if I had delayed another day or so she would have died. I saw my wife's health diminishing after the last emergency room visit and I knew that the doctor that she had was not the one to give us the best results. Prayer and supplications and seeking God on behalf of our loved ones will always give us victory through Christ Jesus. It is so important to have a strong relationship with Him—everyday seeking His will for your life and the life of our loved ones. I developed a serious relationship with the Lord during those trying days. Thanking Him for bringing my wife through this tough time in our lives, my wife endured, pain and suffering, but never did I hear her complain about her condition. She would just say that God will take care of her. Before the operation, I would wake up at night, missing her in the bed, and I would see the light in the hallway on.

I opened the door and said, "Baby, what are you doing up? It's 3:00 a.m. in the morning."

She would reply, "Oh, I wanted to read during the quiet time."

But I knew the real problem – she couldn't breathe. This was the first stage of Congestive Heart Failure. She kept this from me until one night I woke up and missed her again. This time I had to look for her in the house. We had a family room in the basement of the house and I went down there looking for her, and there she was standing up, supporting herself on one of the columns trying to sleep. This broke my heart, but most of all, I was a little upset with her for not telling me of her problem sleeping. She revealed to me, that after I would fall asleep, she would get up and find things to do to stay busy. But God knew that when I would find out about my wife's condition, I would get something done right away.

The doctor that she was seeing was the same doctor treating her sister Minnie Green for heart problems and she had passed in 1998. Praise God for godly wisdom. The next year after her surgery, we decided to celebrate our anniversary in Vancouver, British Columbia. We had to be aware of the medical clinic near the hotel that we stayed so to keep up with the blood test. We went to the clinic and were treated so nice by the Canadian doctor and his staff. We had booked the last two seats on the plane and figured that we could switch with someone so that we can sit together. I went up to the podium and approached the flight attendant, before I could ask her a question about the switch, she said, "I'm not open yet." It was spoken in a very rude tone. So I turned and took my seat. As I sat down, another flight attendant approached the podium. I went back up and asked if I could switch seats with someone. He said, give me your boarding passes. He went on the computer and wrote a new number on our passes.

I looked and it said 3a and 3b. Having flight experience, I knew that this was first class. I said to Gracie, "Look, I think that he changed our seats to first class."

Then he came back to us and said, "Give me those passes again."

I said, "Oh boy."

He came back with printed passes for first-class seats and said, "Stay here until everyone has boarded, then go to the gate. As all the people boarded, he beckoned for us to come forward. The first flight attendant came back to the podium when he went onto the plane. She looked at our boarding pass as if something was wrong, however checking them thoroughly, she admitted us onto the plane in first class, all the way to Vancouver, a six-hour flight. Well, we're treated like the royalty that we are in Christ Jesus.

Here is another example of Divine favor when the enemy is trying to mess up the plan of God for His children. Praise God for favor. Psalms 30:5 says, "His anger endures but for a moment; in His favor is life; weeping may endure for a night, but joy cometh in the morning." He was showing us through this trip, *I've got your back.* The female flight attendant tried to stop us from flying first class, but the male attendant fixed our boarding passes so that she could do nothing but accept the passes. Again, praise God for favor. Those seats would have cost us around $3,000 dollars.

We had a wonderful time together, enjoying the convertible Mustang, going to the most upscale restaurants in Vancouver for dinner each night. We ventured out to Whistler, where the 2010 winter Olympics were to be held. The roads were under construction, but the Rocky Mountains and scenery was so beautiful. One day we went to Grouse Mountain for a Lumber Jack show, that was exciting for Gracie and me to see her smiling and laughing was the best medicine for both of us. I couldn't help but think of my promise to my wife of how I would treat her after my transformation into the man of God that He had ordained me to be. Thank you, Jesus! Going back to the church after vacation time was over, I had a young man in the ministry that was due for ordination as a deacon in the church. His name is Jeffrey Spruill, my daughter's husband. Even though they had been married for only two years at this time, he showed very good stewardship. This young man was no stranger to my family; he grew up from the age of twelve, next door to my mother and siblings on Nairn Place in Newark. He'd always had a crush on Quanika, but she didn't give him the time of day, at first. Sounds familiar. But they got together during her last days at Harvard University. He received the Holy Ghost at Genesis Temple, but he received salvation at House of Prayer some years earlier. What a nice young man he is. His faithfulness paid off in so many ways. Because he is my son-in-law, we became quite close, so much that he began to call me dad. When we would have cookouts at the house, he and Teriq would come over to help set up the tent for the barbeque and tables for the family and church members that would attend.

I was known as the pit master of Lenox Street. Everyone wanted my ribs and steaks. What fellowship that we had in those days. Gracie and my daughters would make salads and desserts. But the grill was mine. The whole family would show up and we would have a wonderful time in the Lord. So we continued in ministry together. By Christmas, my wife and daughters with their families wanted to do something different for that year. So we rented a house down in Orlando, Florida. We all pitched in to help pay for the rental. It was wonderful. We stayed five days and enjoyed our vacation together as a family. My granddaughter had been born and I was busy spoiling her. Amber-Grace, my little princess, as I called her. Quanika and Jeffery didn't have any children as of yet, so I spoiled Dominique and Princess.

After arriving home, I got a message from my sister, Roberta Dukes, that my stepmother was very ill in the hospital and wasn't expected to live much longer. Now I had another challenge to continue with. The Thursday joy night service was in full swing and I received a call telling me to come to the hospital, so I asked my brother to take charge of the service and I went to the hospital to see her for the last time. That morning she passed and now my two siblings by my father, Roberta and Cecil, were looking to me for directions on the funeral. She wanted to be buried in our hometown. This was an additional heartache. I prayed and ask God for directions during this trying time. As I prepared to go to Louisiana to have her home-going service. Now again more pain and heartache, this woman showed me love and compassion when I was a child, but she also showed that same love when I came to live with her and my father in 1966.

So, from that point, the church rallied around me and became more faithful to the ministry. The building fund was also growing as well. One night, a young lady came at the end of our Joy night service and said to me, "Pastor Dukes, my father, who pastors here in Newark has a building for sale on Springfield Avenue, here in the city and want to sell it. It's already a church with two three-bedroom apartments above the church on the second and third floors. I said that I would look at it.

Time went by and I never made any effort to go and see the building; my focuses were on building up the body of Christ and strengthen the members for spiritual warfare. One night, she came back after about two weeks and said, "I thought that you were looking for a building." So I made an appointment with Rev. Shambly, a very well-known Baptist pastor in the city, with a restaurant and buses for hire. I met him at the location, and we went in from the rear parking lot. Upon entering the building, I didn't get too excited about what I was seeing. The building from the outside was okay, but the inside, they had done extensive work in the offices and bathrooms, and the sanctuary was beautiful. All of the pew chairs were blue and it matched the pulpit furniture also matched throughout. There was a fellowship hall on the second floor in the rear of the building with its own tables and chairs included in the sale. The kitchen was very large with a steam table and fridge. I didn't want to get excited because of so many disappointments in the past with different buildings. He told me the price and said that he liked my spirit. Well, this was in 2008 and the economy was in recession.

We had enough for the down payment but needed financing for the balance. He said, "This is what I'm going to do for you and your congregation. I will rent it to you with the purpose of you getting financing."

We'd tried a lot of different banks. Even with good credit, no one would loan us the money, not even the bank that we had been banking with since 1994 – and it was 2008 going into 2009. We had over $100,000 dollars in our building fund and about $10,000 in the regular savings accounts. Still no loan. We moved into the building in October of 2009 and growth took place. As we proceeded to find financing, we were turned down by all banks, including our Bishop's bank. Though all of the calls made to us of prayers and well wishing, we were now up against a wall. The owner was pushing for us to get financing or maybe some other ministry would have to purchase the property. He told me that there was a ministry looking to purchase with cash, but he wanted us to have the building. It had been going on a year now that we had been leasing the building. We never missed a payment and were never late.

One day while working, the Holy Spirit said to me, "Go and have a meeting with him, take Pastor Taylor with you and ask Rev. Shambly to hold the mortgage for you. He has seen that you pay your bills."

Have faith in God! Now I have seen God do some incredible things in my twenty-seven years of walking with Him, so I called and set a meeting asking pop to go with me. Rev. Shambly had met Pop earlier in his restaurant, so he knew him but didn't know that we were connected. At the meeting, after some small talk about church and other things, I ask the pertinent question of holding the mortgage for us. He looked at me and said, "Well, let me talk it over with my board of trustees and I will let you know in about a week." I left the meeting proclaiming victory. I felt the *yes* in my spirit that he would comply with my request of holding the mortgage.

In three days, he called me and said they approved of them holding the mortgage. He would give all the material to his lawyer and she would draw up the papers. I notified my attorney of the process. That Sunday, I didn't have to preach. The Holy Spirit took over the worship service and the praise of God our Father went UN-checked. Here again, God had provided for His people. He has proven to me that He is Jehovah Jireh, the Lord provides. In December of 2010, we closed on the property. The Lord made a way for us to step out on faith in Him down on Washington Street and when we weren't looking for a building, He provided one. We were on Washington Street for twelve years; we went through some trials and testing there as well. It takes being in the furnace awhile and then be delivered by God in order to grow in faith, and move from faith to faith. While we were yet on Washington Street, my brother started his own ministry in South Plainfield, N.J., and went forth as God led him. But God sent me a seasoned Elder. Wayne Peterson came to Genesis as another helper in ministry. What a God that we serve! Later on, Springfield Ave. in the new location, he became my assistant pastor and a great addition to the ministry.

The Lord began to send seasoned people into our ministry as helps. We gained a number of older members, couples as well as new children; ministry goes on here in our new place. By this time, the Lord elevated me to the office of District Superintendent over five other churches. Those pastors worked with me to have a well-organized district. The churches would gather at Genesis and the other churches for our district meetings which would be so powerful with the youth of our district going forth with their talents with praise dance, oratorical skills and also skits or small plays. This was an opportunity for them to show their God-given anointing on their young lives. I believe that when you promote the youth, you are giving them the push that they need to become the church of today and into tomorrow. The great thing about having a separate fellowship hall is that we were able to have free dinners for the ministry every month; this was my way of giving back to the church for their faithfulness.

During the summer months, we would have outreach ministry in the community. We would bring clothes, electronics, and household items to an empty lot down the street from our location. We would rent the lot from the city; the only stipulation was we had to carry insurance for liability purposes. Food and music would draw out people from the community. This would give us the chance to minister to them outside of the walls of the church, where some of them would never come. We would give them a chance to accept Jesus Christ as their redeemer. Then we would send a team of seasoned saints out on Saturdays with what we called *door knockers*, talking to whoever would open their doors to us. Then we would stand in front of the church building and give out bottles of cold water on hot days. This drew people into the ministry. We were situated on a main street and bus line so people would come to church on Sundays by bus.

I believe that this method of reaching people where they were worked well for us and the ministry flourished. In 2008, I became a Newark Police Chaplain with responsibilities to work in the U.M.D.N.J. now known as Rutgers Medical Center. Every week I would volunteer for Chaplaincy duty in the evening and go on patrol with the detectives of the force. This gave me the opportunity to interact with city officials and ranking police. We were officiating over recruit graduations and ceremonies, as well as when retired or active duty officers would retire and their funerals. I enjoyed my position as a vice-chairman of the Clergy Alliance that was connected to all of the wards in the city. I had the lower half of the West Ward and sheared the downtown area with another pastor. During the summer months, he would have youth from upper Michigan and Minnesota. They would come to the city to learn how inner-city people lived and fellowshipped. He would bring them to our church and they would help us clean the neighborhood, cut grass in the empty lot where we would have our outreach on Saturdays. These were good young people. I would take them on tours of the city, giving them the story of the 1967 riots and then feed them lunch before they returned to their church for the evening. It was an experience to minister to youth from a totally different culture and backgrounds. They interacted very well with us. They'd tell us how much they enjoyed the work and fellowship. Soon the church would be packed out on Sundays. The sanctuary held around 200 people and, most Sundays, we would have at least 150-160 worshippers, this gave me the boost to stay in the Word and before God, seeking His guidance for ministry directions.

During one Sunday afternoon service, just as the speaker was finishing up her message, I looked at my wife and she had a strange look on her face. She was staring into space. I knew something was wrong. A few weeks earlier, the doctors had installed a defibrillator pacemaker in her chest, and what I was seeing was the device going off, her heart had stopped and it kicked in. I gently got up from my seat in the pulpit and went over to her without drawing a lot of attention. I placed my hands on her face and she came out of the stare, and said, "Oh, I must have fallen asleep." I thought from her looks that she had a stroke, but praise God it wasn't so. Of course, this ended the service anyway, especially when EMS showed up. The amazing thing was that she was alright for the moment, she refused to go to the hospital, but that evening when we returned home, the hospital called. She was connected by the device in our bedroom, which read her attack. They wanted her to come in for a readjustment of the device. I knew that my wife's heart was giving out on her. Every time we went to see the cardiologist, he would say her heart has lost more strength.

My daughters and I set a meeting with him to discuss a heart transplant. He wasn't too excited about that for her because of the weakness of her body, but we didn't know at the time, was that she had major lung problems as well. She had other underlying issues. But through her illness, she never once complained, nor did she mumble about her breathing issues. She worked harder than anyone in the church as far as ministry duties. She would have monthly meetings with the women of the church and would chair programs.

I tried to slow her down, and she would get upset with me and say, "I've got to do the work of the church while I can."

When her health started to fail, I asked her to stay home from the business and let Ishia run the office. She would go by sometimes and check on her, but didn't do any work. I saw the need for me to retire and take care of my Gracie. I ask the Lord to allow me to do this. Before retiring from Wings Pest Control, the Lord told me to start paying down debts. Credit cards, revolving cards like Macy's and other debts that I could handle. This took a process of elimination. I turned sixty-two years old in May of 2011 and had my ducks in order.

I had by then informed my employees that I was selling the company and already had a buyer lined up that wanted the high-end clientele that we had accumulated over the years. Some had been with us as long as twenty years. They knew that one day this would happen because I had discussed it with them previously.

By August of 2011, I had things in motion and the Lord was in the process as well. Everything went so smoothly with the process of change. As a professional company, we had all of our documents in order, by November of 2011, the business was sold and we had the closing of our office on Sanford Ave., Newark, N.J., a few blocks from my home. Now I could give my time to my responsibilities as pastor and caretaker for my wife. One day she started to complain about the steps in the house and how it was getting more difficult for her to negotiate the stairs every day. She would go upstairs and stay. I had a house-keeper come in to take care of the washing and cleaning of the house. This bothered my wife immensely, because she was a very good housewife.

One day she said to me, "Walter this house is killing me. You've got to put it on the market. I know that we have lived here for thirty years and you are attached to this house with all of its memories, but we've got to go."

I knew then that I had to put our home on the market because she meant more to me than the house. The first realtor that we contacted had some very good photos taken of all of the rooms. Over the years, we had done some very fine upgrades to the basement, bedrooms, and kitchen with high-end cabinets and appliances. People would come and be in awe over the house, but didn't want to pay our price for it. At this time houses in our community values had increased tremendously and because of the upgrades that we had done, we didn't back down on our price. After a while, there were no more lookers so we took it off the market for a year. By 2013, we put it back on and got a serious buyer that wanted the house and gave us our price for it.

By now, pastor and Mother Taylor had moved out of N.J. and down to Delaware to live, commuting back up on weekends for worship services going back on Sunday nights. We had been visiting them on occasions and liked Delaware as well. After looking around in N.J. for condos and retirement communities, everything that we looked at in nice communities was way out of our budget. New Jersey is one of the most expensive states to retire in, except maybe California. So, Pop had to go into the hospital for a procedure and we went down to see him. The medical staff treated him so well and I observed the treatment for myself. Gracie said to me on the way back up to Jersey, maybe we should move down here. After looking around in Jersey, and seeing the cost of living for us, I prayed and asked the Lord for directions. The buyer for the house had some issues to handle before we could move forward on the sale.

We heard from the Lord and what He spoke into my spirit was, *First look at the medical support for your wife.* This gave me a lot of thought. When I would take her to the clinic for her two-week blood check, I would take my devotional books and the newspaper, waiting outside in the car, or going to the car wash or supermarket. After about one and half hours of waiting, she would emerge from the clinic looking tired from the rigors of being in there with so many people. So, we started looking online in Delaware for condos for lease, we didn't want to purchase another home because of her health.

One of the greatest challenges in this move would be the ministry. It would be a real challenge from where Pop and Mom Taylor lived. So we looked up near the bridge. We found a condo in Bear, DE. It was really nice, two bedrooms with an office and dining area, upgraded carpet and crown molding in the living room, dining room and office. This was just what we are looking for.

In Jersey, this unit would lease for close to $2500 a month without garage rent. Here in Bear, we got both for $1600 a month. Now here is the challenge for ministry. It was exactly 118 miles from the front door to the rear door of the church, a total of 236 miles round trip. So my oldest daughter fixed up a room for us and we would come up on Thursdays for Joy Night and stay with her and her family until Sunday after worship. Now that we had this condo in Delaware and limited stairs for my wife to go up and down, we started looking for doctors and clinics to take her on as a patient. The cardiologist had a lab in his office for her INR blood checks every two weeks. The first time that we went to the office, I took my devotional book and the newspaper. I settled down in the car for some reading and after about ten minutes, Gracie emerged from the building with a paper in her hand. I asked, "What happened?"

She said, "I'm finished. Here are my results."

Wow, what a change from Jersey. The doctor took real good care of her. I began to see the advantage of living here. The condo and area that it was located in was so nice. We had lived in the city for so long, that moving here in the country, so to speak, was so different. The pharmacy was just up the road and so were all of the stores. This made my wife so happy. I could see right away that we'd made a good choice for her. I know that God was in the plan.

This was the spring of 2014 and everything was going smoothly until one day, my brother called me and said our mother was in the hospital with congestive heart failure. I knew about this disease all too well. We went up to the hospital to see her and all of my siblings was present and accounted for except Dorothy, who lived in Texas. We prayed together for Momma and the family. We've been through some tough times together with the loss of our eldest sister Donnell in 2002, the same time and year of Quanika's and Jeffrey's wedding. Now our mother was sick, she was in her eighties and very weak in her body. My youngest sister Monica was taking care of her in her home and doing a great job of it. After returning back to Delaware, Gracie started having some real breathing problems, so the doctor ordered her oxygen machine and long lines to move around in the house. By this time, my mother was getting worse in her health as well. What challenges this was for my siblings and me.

March of 2015, my mother passed and all of our family from all over the country came to Newark for the home going service. My mother was well-loved throughout the Jersey brotherhood of churches. The Well's Cathedral Church, which holds about 1200 people was filled with family and well-wishers just as Pop Pringle's home-going service. I had in my ministry officiated over a number of home goings in this beautiful Cathedral and often thought as I waited to do the eulogy. One day I would be sitting out there where this family is mourning their loved one, and sure enough, it's my and my family's turn to mourn our mother's passing from this life to the next. What gave us so much comfort was that we knew that she had a relationship

135

with Jesus Christ and she was a godly woman who read her Bible every day.

My mother didn't raise me, but I had a good relationship with her. It was due to her prayers and others that brought about my change. I had the opportunity to see her happy after marrying Elder Henry Pringle. He treated her in such a way I'm sure she'd wanted to be treated earlier in her life. But God knows when, where, and how He will bring our blessings to fruition. She never married again after his death, even though she was at the time still young enough to do so. She made her life her children and ministry. Thank God for Momma! The summer of 2015 came and I told my family that we would go down to Louisiana to visit my hometown. My grands had never been neither had my son-in-law. We rented a large comfort van that would accommodate all of us. At this time, Gracie was not all that great and I was concerned about the long road trip for her, but she insisted that she would be fine. Quanika, Jeffrey, Ishia, Amber-Grace, Rico, Jeffrey Jr., and Jacob, along with Gracie and me, embarked upon this journey together as a family. We had a wonderful time on the road, stopping for fuel and food only.

My thoughts for taking this trip was twofold. The first thing was so that my grandchildren would see where I was born and to meet their cousins. The second was so that the people that said I would never amount to anything could see at my age, how I turned out and what I was able to accomplish in life, God being my guide and my helper. Previously to this trip, I had been to my hometown on a number of occasions for different purposes. One time that rings clear, and it seems to bear truth, that most of my visits were for loved one's home-going services.

In 2000 my first cousin, Ezzard, was killed in a terrible automobile accident and then other family members were lost. Ezzard's death really bothered me because we were close in age and relationship; we were two sister's children. His mother, Mary Louise, is the aunt that I mentioned earlier in my writing. She was the oldest sister of my mother's siblings. Mary Louise passed in 2009 and I was privileged to eulogize her at the request of my other cousins, Glenda, Jackie, and Philip were the remaining siblings.

So for me to go back now for pleasure was very good therapy for all of us. We arrived in Natchitoches and went to our hotel and then to Glenda's home. The first day we toured the small town, which now is a tourist attraction with a French flavor. The children enjoyed seeing a river going through the midst of downtown, very beautiful. There were still some of the elderly people living in the same homes that they did when I was a child growing up. They would say to me, "Boy, you are a bad little boy," and I was very mischievous. But God had His hands on me. The vision that God gave to me in this little town of having a wife, two children, a good job, a nice car, and by the time that I would reach thirty, I would have a home.

All of the vision had come to pass and the Holy Spirit reminded me of the vision that God gave me to repeat to myself. My wife and I had now been married for forty-five years and were still very much in love with each other. I would tell her every day how much that I loved her, especially now that I knew her health was failing fast. We went to visit some of the elderly people and they were so surprised to see my family and me. They talked about my childhood and, after I told them that I was a pastor and business owner, they were so impressed with my success in life. That Sunday, my cousins had me preach at their church, the church that I grew up going to. A few of the old classmates came as well as some of the older people from the neighborhood. The service was very good and the Lord blessed one lady to give her life to Christ. That in itself, made the trip worthwhile. To God be the glory!

When we returned back home it was such a good trip for all of us that we looked at all of the pictures that were taken in my hometown and rejoiced that God had allowed us to complete it. However, my wife was not breathing well and the doctor sent her to a specialist in pulmonology. They did x-rays and scans on her; her heart was getting weaker and weaker. She was admitted a couple of times in the hospital just for breathing treatments. This would be so upsetting to watch my wife trying to breathe.

I'm writing this to help someone who is a caretaker for a loved one, to encourage you to hold on to your relationship with the Lord. Through Viet Nam and the streets, nothing hurt me more than to see my wife, the love of my life suffer this way. As she began her journey towards the end of life, my prayers for her, was *Lord ease the pain and suffering, please Lord.* God spoke into my spirit and told me that he was going to receive her soon. When He told me this, I would go into the living room and just weep and cry so profusely asking God to strengthen me for this time of our lives. I would clean, shop for groceries, and make her as comfortable as possible. Then the last hospital visit for breathing, the doctors said that we have to put a catheter into her arm going into her heart with a drug that would keep her heart pumping. The nurse came to our house to give me instructions on how to change the bag every seventy-two hours and how to clean and sanitize the catheter with heparin flushes. This was a lot to absorb.

We met with the cardiologist and pulmonologist specialists and they both suggested a heart transplant at this time. I spoke to my wife about this when we went back home and she said, "Okay, let's look into it."

Again, I want to tell this part of my life to encourage someone that might read my story and gain a little more faith in our God. Every day I would get up real early, spend time with the Lord in prayer and supplication with devotional time in His Word. This is the method and only method of getting through storms of life is by staying in the face of God, seeking Him on a daily basis, not just asking for miracles, but sending up praise and worship with thanksgiving. Yes, this was the most difficult time in our lives.

Gracie, with tubes, and about fourteen drugs, and oxygen tanks in the house, never once uttered a complaint that I could hear. I would tell her how much I admired her faith in God, and she would just say, "I belong to Him and He will take care of me."

When it was time to go up to Jersey for ministry, I would say, "Honey, why don't you let me ask our neighbor to come over to be with you while I go up to minister and come back after worship?"

She would just say, "No way am I staying home while you go by yourself."

By the time we got to this stage of our lives, the doctors didn't want her to travel for two hours up to Jersey, but she insisted on going, so they said okay, but that I had to stop a few times on the Turnpike for her to get out and move around a little. By this time, we were only going up on Sundays and this had a great effect on ministry as you would expect it to. Members started leaving and the church activities diminished to just Sunday worship. I prayed and asked God, *Lord, what am I going to do? I can't be in two places at one time.* Yes, I had an executive pastor, but when the senior pastor was not functioning at full capacity, things go undone.

I heard a word from the Lord that encouraged me, and He said to me, "Take care of your wife, be the best caretaker for her, don't worry over the church, I will handle it. You do your best to make my maid servant comfortable."

The doctor said that I have three different hospitals to recommend to you for the transplant. We chose John Hopkins because it was the closest to us, only sixty miles away in Baltimore, Maryland. We called and set up a consultation with the head cardiologist and the tests began for her to see if she could undergo this super major operation. The first test went alright and after two other visits, the lungs had to be tested. Gracie was a strong trooper to go through this entire test, some being intrusive, never once did she complain. So, we drove back down to the hospital for the lung part of the exams. By the way, the hospital and staff at Christiana Medical hospital treated Gracie as if she was the Queen of England and the staff of John Hopkins did the same. The nurse came into the waiting room and called her in. Within about a half-hour she came out, and I could tell by the look on her face that things didn't go so well. I ask her what happened, and she said, "I couldn't blow into the machine to measure my lung strength, so they are sending me back to the cardiologist doctor."

We made another appointment and the doctor asked my wife, "Mrs. Dukes have you ever smoked cigarettes?"

She answered, "No."

"Have you worked in an industrial environment?

She answered, "No."

"Well, your lungs look like someone that has smoked two packs of cigarettes for thirty years."

We looked at each other in disbelief and we knew what that meant. I asked the doctor what bearing did this have on the transplant. He said we will re-evaluate the case and call you in a few days.

On the way home, Gracie spoke, after we rode up the highway awhile. "Walter, I didn't ask for this transplant anyway, I belong to God and He will take care of me. I was so depressed and despondent over the news."

After two days, the doctor called with the news and said that he was so sorry to be the bearer of this news, but the transplant was off and that the doctors from Christiana would be calling with a follow-up appointment, and sure enough, the surgeon from the hospital called.

That weekend we had gone up to Jersey for our spring workers meeting of 2016 and, before we left home, I changed the Milrinone bag so it should be good for seventy-two hours. The drug was pumped into the heart by a portable pump that has a loud alarm if the pump stops working or the drug runs out. We went to the meeting that Friday night and everything was fine, but I noticed she didn't look so good on Saturday, but she insisted that she was fine.

By Sunday on the way home, she was sleeping a lot and lethargic in movement. On Monday morning it was time to change the pouch. To my surprise, when I opened the pouch that housed the pump and drug, the bag was still full. The pump malfunctioned and hadn't sounded the alarm. I was very upset over this. We had the appointment at the hospital and we rushed to the hospital in a panic. The surgeon took one look at her and sent us directly to the E.R. When they checked her Inr, that's the thickness of her blood, it was so thin that if she had scratched herself she would have bled to death. It took them four days to get it back to normal.

We met with the doctors and they said, "It's time for hospice. We can do nothing more at this time for your wife."

She sat there in the wheelchair and just listened to what they were saying.

"This doesn't mean that you are going to die right away, Mrs. Dukes, it just means we are turning you over to another mode of more intense observance."

We received all kinds of medical equipment, some attached to the telephone and there were other medical duties assigned to me on a daily bases. She would have a nurse and aide come every day for checkups. The aide would help her with her hair and such, but that was all she had to do, most of the time she was company for her. Everyone that came to our home loved my Gracie; she was a very likeable person, with a sweet disposition. As 2016 rolled along, she was doing so well on this drug, that she wanted me to push her around in the mall to look at clothes in Macy's Department store. She asked the hospice doctor if she could fly. Gracie loved to travel and she wanted to go back out to California to visit my relatives.

She and my uncle Richard's wife, Dianne, were very close and got along like sisters. The doctor said to her, "Mrs. Dukes, we can sign off on you flying, but we can't be responsible for anything happening to you while flying or out there. It's possible that you can have an embolism while flying that distance."

She looked at me and I shook my head no. We didn't take that chance. One of the advice that the doctors at John Hopkins informed us, it was because of her weakened immune system, to limit people hugging and kissing her. We were aware of this for a while and as the year came to a close, my daughters and their families would come down to visit us more frequently.

By the time her sixty-fourth birthday came in November of 2016, she was doing as well as expected. The nurse and hospice doctor were amazed at her will to live and that she was doing so well on the heart drug. Christmas was spent with our children and grands. All of them loving on Nanna as they would call her. My whole life was taking care of her needs and attending to her. The New Year came in, 2017 and by now, everywhere we went, I had to pack the wheelchair for her. Oh, it gave me an honor to push her around in the store. One of her favorite stores was Ross and by now, she only purchased things for our granddaughter, Amber-Grace.

This time reminded me of our traveling together and on a day that she was feeling well enough, we would talk about trips that we took and watch tapes and DVDs from those vacations. One, in particular, was the 2005 cruise to the Mediterranean, Italy, Spain, the Canary Islands, Morocco, and an island called Madeira Funchal off the coast of Portugal. What a trip it was. It lasted for fifteen days and we had such a wonderful time. Now at this stage of our lives, she couldn't travel anymore. But memories filled our days. Going up to Jersey seeing our children and grands would brighten her spirits. The church was very much on my mind and I prayed to God as I saw the time approaching.

Lord, what do I do? Show me, my Lord, how to go forward in ministry when I am taking care of a sick wife and trying to minister to your sheep in Jersey. My constant prayer was, *Lord I need your help in this hour of our lives, help me to do my duty as a husband who loves his wife and as a pastor who loves the members as well.* I would cry sometimes as we traveled up to Jersey. I would look over at her in the car on our way up; she would sleep all the way and would not see me crying, because of what I saw in the spirit realm. My Lord, how long will I have her with me? May came and Mother's Day came. Gracie loved to dress; she was a First Lady in every area of the title. Our daughters thought of buying her a special dress for the day. She looked so beautiful in the dress, even though she had lost so much weight from a loss of appetite. We celebrated her in a very special way. My birthday came and at this time the meds were not working so well, and she had a lot of bad nights. I administered morphine to her for pain and comfort. Hospice would come and check her vitals. The week before Father's day, Pop and Mom Taylor came up to Bear for a visit and asked if she felt good enough to go to Roadhouse Restaurant for dinner. She said, "Yes, it's only right up the street from our house." She ate only a little salad and was quiet during dinner.

The day was Tuesday, and Tuesday was sale day at Ross. Pop was teasing her and asked her if she wanted to go to the store and she said *no*. So after the dinner was over, we went back to our clubhouse in our complex and sat by the pool for some spring air. My Gracie was slipping away from me; I could see her fading as she would just sit and look into nothing. One night before Father's Day, I got in bed with her and she began to talk. She said, "Walter, you are a good man, and you have made me so happy as your wife. You have given me so much joy and happiness. I just want to thank you for what you do and how you show me your love."

I turned over and said to myself, "*Why is she telling me this now? Lord is this the time*"? That Friday, she was feeling well enough to go up to Jersey for the last time. After Sunday morning worship, we went to one of our favorite restaurants in Jersey, all our family was present. Gracie picked over her salad and didn't eat any of her meal. The hospice nurse had told me a while ago, that when I see that loss of appetite, it's part of the ending of life and her organs are starting to shut down.

We went outside of the restaurant to take pictures for Father's Day memories. This would be the last photo that we would take together. Our children said goodbye and we got on the road back to Delaware. She slept all the way home. The next week she started feeling worse, all that week, heavy on the meds and she didn't want to eat. I would fix her breakfast and she would only pick over it, so I would make her favorite thing, fruit salad, but still, she wouldn't eat but a little.

That Saturday night she was having a lot of complications breathing, so I called the emergency hospice nurse and she came right away and I took the med box from the fridge and she administered the special meds for her to calm her breathing. I observed how she was looking at my wife and I knew from her look that my Gracie was in trouble. I had to pick her up to take her into the bathroom and to wash her up for bed. She couldn't lay flat in the bed, so I put her in the chair and that's where she stayed all night.

Sunday morning, I knew that I couldn't go up to Jersey, so I called my executive pastor and informed him. The service went on as scheduled. The saints were led into prayer for their first lady by him, and all who attended. I was under a tremendous amount of stress and anxiety. Watching the woman that I've loved my whole youth and adult life suffer and all I could do was take the best care of her that I knew how. We got through Sunday and Sunday night.

Monday morning, the aide and nurse came to see about her and when they walked into our home, the nurse said, "I'm calling the hospital for transport, she's in big trouble."

The aide said to me, "I can't believe how much she's gone down since Friday."

The ambulance came, and I thought that I was taking her to get better and then bring her home again, but that wasn't the case. They sedated her. My daughters were on the road that morning coming down, because they knew that something was drastically wrong if Dad didn't come up for service Sunday morning. Just as she was about to go to sleep, they arrived and when Ishia, my youngest daughter, came into the room, she fainted and the nurses came running in to assist her. She recovered and all of my grands came in and we communed as a family, with Pop and Mom Taylor by our side for support.

We arrived at the hospital at around noon time and by six-something that evening, she was gone to glory as I held her in my arms. I said it was okay to leave now and go home to glory. We were also accompanied by her niece, Sheryl and her husband Donald, they were on their way home from Jersey to Virginia and was going to stop by our home for a visit and found out that she had been hospitalized. My daughter Quanika was quiet and I knew that she was going through some very hard pain, so when we got back to my place, she exploded with a scream that I will never forget. I'm sure my neighbors heard her and figured something tragic had happened, because every one of them knew of my wife's health challenges. We spent the evening consoling each other. This was one of the worst days of my life. Nothing compared to this, not even my mother's, father's or stepdad's death hit me like this.

The pain was and is indescribable; I wouldn't want anyone to experience the pain that I felt. My wife and best friend was gone, and now, I'm alone. She went to glory on June 26th 2017, one day before our forty-seventh wedding anniversary, which made it just the more painful. I cried out to God for help and relief from the pain. He first reminded me that He had mercy upon me when He informed me earlier in the year that He would receive her soon, and that she just slept away with me holding her in my arms. My relationship with God got stronger from that point.

As before her death, I meet the Lord every morning in prayer and devotional time and the thought never entered my mind to blame Him or accuse anyone for my pain. The home-going arrangements were made with the funeral parlor in Jersey for the week after the fourth of July celebrations so that all of my family and her family came to make their plans to attend. I went up to Jersey to spend this time with my family and church members. They felt so bad over the loss of the first lady. They cried as profusely as did I. The time came, and all of my family arrived, from as far as California, Louisiana, Georgia, Texas, and Virginia.

They came to support me, my family, not just because they loved me, but because of their love of Gracie. She was just that kind of person, firm but loving and sweet at the same time. Oh, what a woman. Well-wishers from all over the brotherhood attended her home going services. Bishops and Jurisdictional supervisors alike came to say their farewells to Sister Dukes, as she was known in the church body. Our Jurisdictional Bishop, Norman Prescott gave the message of healing and comfort to us, and as I sat there, the Holy Spirit reminded me of the times that I gave words of comfort and healing on so many occasions. Now it was my turn to be comforted. The church could not hold all of the well-wishers and visitors, so it was a steady flow of people coming in and out of the church until the service began. My daughters and grands held up pretty good until the closing of the casket. We all went through a tremendous amount of pain and anguish that day after the repass had ended. Her lying away was to take place in Delaware Veteran's Cemetery the next day. I held up fairly well until everybody had gone back home and back to their lives.

When the hospice team came to clear out the equipment and medications that were left over from her treatments. Then it hit me. I'm alone for the first time in my adult life. I had lost the best thing that ever has happened to me in my whole life, except being born again. Gracie was my best friend. All of the memories started flooding my mind, from the first date and first kiss to our first-born child. Being retired I had nothing but time on my hands. I would get up early in the morning and have my devotional time with the Lord, praying and crying out to Him for help in my grief. I can't describe the pain.

Then I would go to the gym and work out for two hours, trying to get some relief. I would find myself weeping in the middle of my work out. The next Sunday, I was in my church ministering to the church even though I was in extreme pain, I still did my job as a pastor. I felt that I had to minister in order to be healed myself and it did help. But I needed professional help, I found myself going to the cemetery weekly and weeping over her grave. The Veteran's Cemetery was like a park with a pond and ducks and benches to sit on. My heart would be so heavy that I could barely see the road on my way back to an empty condo.

Then one day, after about a month of going out there, the Holy Spirit spoke to me while standing over her grave. He said, "Walter, this is no good, you need to stop coming out here; she's not here, she's with Jesus."

So I stayed away as much as I could. Then I heard about a program in grief counseling at one of the local churches, so I made an appointment and took the classes in grief and mourning behaviors. It did me a lot of good to know that there were other people hurting like me and seeking help. The counselors were all PHDs in their fields and offered sound wisdom and advice to the class. I attended four sessions and felt the Lord strengthen me in the process. I would go down to visit Mom and Pop Taylor in Smyrna and they would treat me so wonderful, having prayer with me before leaving. Having family and close friends is good during that time, but it was God who brought me through the most trying time of my life.

In August of 2017, I decided that I needed to get away from my environment and went out to my favorite state in the country, California. My memories of living there prompted me to go for a visit with my uncles and their families. They have shown me so much love and did love my Gracie as a sister. Arriving in Long Beach, I stayed at Richard's house. This uncle is more like my younger brother than an uncle, being that I'm almost three years older than he. We grew up together and have always been close.

After being there a few days, one day I decided, after coming from the gym, that I would drive down to San Clemente and on to Camp Pendleton. I started out on the 405-freeway going south and after about a mile, every memory of Gracie flooded my mind at one time and I felt my mind leaving me, I yelled out JESUS! And the sensation lifted immediately and I drove on. Now weeping and sobbing over this experience, my day was over. Yes, I drove down to San Clemente and went by the places that we had lived, but instead of bringing me good feelings, it only increased my grief over her. On down to Pendleton, I was still in this cloud and not enjoying myself, perhaps if I had someone with me, it would not have been so bad. My uncle and aunt had to work that day, so it wasn't possible for them to go. I made it back to Long Beach and sat on his patio crying over the bad experience of the day.

Jesus saved my mind from leaving me. When I yelled His name, I could feel my mind coming back down like a thermometer. I praise God for my relationship with Him; He has saved me more times than I can count. He is a mind regulator and heart fixer, problem solver, He is God. I know that some people might feel that I was maybe too close to her, but I read a Scripture in Ephesians 5:25 that says, "Husbands love your wives, just as Christ also loved the church and gave Himself for her."

When I was young in the Word and couldn't understand how I could love my wife this way, but believed that one day with the Lord's help I could love her that way. The last ten years of our lives together and maturing in the Word, growing in grace and in the knowledge of our Lord and Savior Jesus Christ, I began to live this Scripture. Yes, a husband can love his wife that much! I loved her with a love that will always be in my heart. My daughters and grandchildren began to draw closer to me, calling on a daily basis, checking on me, and when I would go up to Jersey, they would pour love on me. In my darkest hour of pain, their faces would come before me.

I exclaimed to God, "Lord, please take away this pain that I'm feeling, and if not, my Lord bring me to where she is." Then the Lord would remind me of what I have to live for. *First and foremost, you have a family that loves you and needs you now, your youngest daughter Ishia is hurting as you are, and she needs her dad. Quanika the rock need you as well even though she does not show her emotions on the outside, inside she's hurting as well and don't forget about your little princess Amber-Grace. Walter, the church is looking to you for strength as well.*

So when the Lord spoke these words into my spirit, I began to just praise and give thanksgiving to Him, saying, yes, Lord! Help me to get through this time in my life. A very dark time when nothing seemed to bring me much joy. When I would slip into a depression, my group that I met with at the VA would encourage me as well, friends would call and check on me as well. Bishop Cahoon, my former pastor, would call and have prayer with me. He knew all too well of the pain that I was in because earlier on he had lost the love of his life. So he knew just how to minister to me.

Thank God for men and women of God. I drew strength from all of the saints that knew my wife and our ministry! I am so proud of my daughters. My eldest, Quanika, has three degrees. She attended Mount Ida College, Harvard University, and Seaton Hall University. She has accomplished a lot in her life, and now an executive with the Newark Board of Education. Ishia, my youngest, is a classroom teacher with both behavioral and music being her strong suit.

Out of this little country boy from a small town in Louisiana comes two educators and five grandchildren that are on the way to accomplishing great things in their lives. But if God had not changed the course of my direction when I was thirty-one, I don't think that these things would have come to pass and the old prophesies would have been true about that little red-headed boy name Lil' Duke. But for God!

To be continued...

Gracie and I at a banquet a year before her death.